THE HORROR OF DRACULA

THE HORROR OF DRACULA

Screenplay
By
Jimmy Sangster

Production Background
By
Ronald V. Borst

Edited
By
Philip J Riley

Also contains "The Vampyre"
By John Polidori, 1819
With an introduction by Michael Hartley

Classic Hammer Film Series
MagicImage Filmbooks is an
imprint of BearManor Media

MagicImage Filmbooks is an imprint of:

BearManor Media
P.O. Box 1129
Duncan, OK 73534-1129

Phone: 580-252-3547
Fax: 814-690-1559

©2013 Philip J Riley
For Copyright purposes
No copyright is implied on the shooting script
Philip J. Riley is the author in the form of this book

Horror of Dracula - An Analysis of the Hammer Film Classic by Ronald V. Borst
first appeared in Mark Franks's *PHOTON*, Issue 27, 1977
 - revised 2013 © Ronald V. Borst
Horror of Dracula - Screenplay by Jimmy Sangster
Horror of Dracula, the film released in 1958 - Made by Hammer Studios
Script courtesy of Richard A. Ekstedt used with permission of Jimmy Sangster
Pressbook Courtesy of Ronald V. Borst/Hollywood Movie Posters
Photographs Courtesy - William Forsche and Ronald V. Borst and the Editor

Editor's note: In Jimmy Sangster's script Van Helsing is called Hesling and Jonathan Harker is called Jonathon Harker. Also the original punctuation, British slang words and spelling are as they existed in the original document. It was set in Prestige Elite type to match the original.

Whenever possible photographs and poster are not cropped for historic reasons.

First BearManor Media edition 2013

The purpose of this series is the preservation of the art of writing for the screen. Rare books have long been a source of enjoyment and an investment for the serious collector, and even in limited editions there are thousands printed. Scripts, however, numbered only 50 at the most. In the history of American Literature, the screenwriter was being lost in time. It is my hope that my efforts bring about a renewed history and preservation of a great American Literary form, The Screenplay, by preserving them for study by future generations.

Dedicated to Sir Christopher Lee

PRODUCTION BACKGROUND
By
Ronald V. Borst

The early spring of 1957 saw the New York City arrival of James Carreras, then managing director of Britain's modest Hammer Films Ltd. Accompanying him on his flight to the United States were his twenty-nine year-old son, Michael, Hammer's executive producer, and the company's producer, thirty-five year old Anthony Hinds.

With them they had brought newly filmed sequences from their unfinished production, *The Curse of Frankenstein*. Unable to secure the financial support of a major Hollywood distributor in the making of the movie, the British trio now sought to secure a contractual agreement with Warner Brothers whereby Warners would handle the worldwide distribution of their first color horror film. The Warner executives who screened the segments were sufficiently impressed with the footage that a mutual agreement which satisfied both parties was soon concluded and the Englishmen returned home, elated over the financial prospects their latest project promised to bring them. *The Curse of Frankenstein* was completed shortly thereafter premiering in London on May 2, 1957 and going on to become Hammer's biggest money-maker up to that time. But even before that film was released initial plans for a follow-up were being discussed should the new *Frankenstein* prove as profitable as expected. As the Laemmles of Universal had turned to *Frankenstein* after the unexpected phenomenal success of *Dracula*, no now did the Carreras' turn to Bram Stoker's vampire novel, unknowingly launching a film project which would ultimately emerge as their company's finest and most famous production—*Horror of Dracula*.

Bela Lugosi as Dracula, Universal 1931

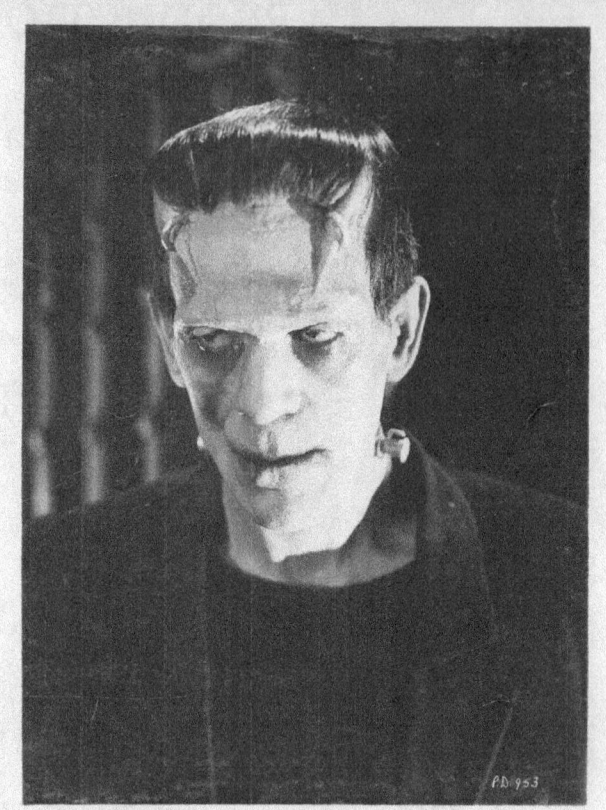

Boris Karloff as Frankenstein's Monster, Universal 1931

Unlike the Shelley classic, *Dracula* had yet to receive a "definitive" screen treatment. While one may fault Whale's *Frankenstein* for being somewhat dated, melodramatic and unfaithful rendition of the original 1916 novel, Karloff's portrayal of the Monster in makeup design by Jack Pierce has made the film so singularly unique that it is unlikely ever to be equalled, let alone surpassed. However, with *Dracula* there have been three excellent adaptations, each one pointedly different in style and approach. Murnau's *Nosferatu*, the first and illegally produced version of 1922 was obviously never intended to be a faithful or realistic adaptation. Drastically altering Stoker's novel, Murnau's characters emerge not so much as human as they do bizarre and unnatural shadow-like beings existing in an expressionistic world during a time and place that seems difficult to imagine could ever have existed.

Browning's *Dracula* should have been the equal to Whale's *Frankenstein*, it might have been had Laemmle Jr. chosen to utilize an earlier screenplay written by Louis Bromfield—a script which adhered far more closely to the novel and from which only the first sequences in Transylvania were retained. Coupled with more spirited direction and pacing the film would have transcended the plodding stage play it ultimately became. As it remains, the film is cherished for its first fifteen minutes, its memorable lines, and for Lugosi's classic interpretation which suited the kind of film Browning fashioned.

Disregarding an apparently lost Hungarian *Drakula* of 1921, *the Spanish language version of Universal's* Dracula, and the minor *Drakula Instanbulda* variation on the novel (1953), there remain but three other noteworthy versions *Horror of Dracula*, Jesus Franco's *Count Dracula* (1970, and Dan Curtis' *Dracula* (1974). While the Franco film may have allowed Christopher Lee the opportunity to physically interpret the vampire along the lines of the author's descriptions, the effort was shoddily mounted and ineptly directed with its best moments often ruined by utterly amateurish camerawork, relying heavily on zoom effects. Curtis' *Dracula*—premiering on American television and theatrically released abroad—contained some beautiful and atmospheric location photography and some equally fine attention to period detail. However, by attempting to inject an overly sympathetic approach to its title character (a theme visually reinforced by some outlandishly trite soap opera flashbacks in slow motion) it became a sort of cross between Cutis' best vampire film, *The Night Stalker*, and his worst, *House of Dark Shadows*. Like the Franco film, Curtis' *Dracula* is often hampered through its abominable overuse of the zoom and little can be said of the production's prolonged and badly staged finale other than that it ranks with the equally bliase climaxes of the Murnau, Browning and Franco films.

With the success of The Curse of Frankenstein - Hammer reteamed its two new horror stars - Christopher Lee and Peter Cushing

Horror of Dracula is certainly as unfaithful in its adaptation as any of the other versions yet produced, if not moreso admittedly, it also lacks the Gothic styled atmosphere prevalent in the Murnau and Browning films. And yet, there is little question that it represents the finest version of Dracula from the standpoint of realism, action, eroticism and pacing. "The chemistry of Jimmy Sangster's script, the entire cast and crew...everything about the first *Dracula* seemed to mesh perfectly." Terence Fisher has reiterated this statement in one form or another in various interviews over the years and it still best sums up the major reasons for the film's financial success as we as its ever-increasing international popularity.

Unlike *Curse of the Demon*, (UK title *Night of the Demon*) 1958's other outstanding supernatural thriller and a production which was considerably marred through producer interference. Fisher's *Dracula* was fortunately blessed with producers who continually enhanced the production through its developmental stages. Much of its success can be attributed to the kind of company Hammer had become by the time they decided to remake both *Frankenstein* and *Dracula*. Although its name (from co-founder Will Hammer, aka William Hinds) predated World War II, it was not until after the war's end when the company reformed as a subsidiary production company under Exclusive Films that the modern-day Hammer Film Productions Ltd. actually took root. Exclusive/Hammer gradually came to prominence in the fifties producing their own dramas, comedies, swashbucklers, etc., as well as the fir British science fiction films of the decade, *Four-Sided Triangle* and *Spaceways* (both 1953). The company did additional business by reissuing old films and by co-producing with America's Lippert Pictures. Throughout those early days of the fifties, Exclusive/Hammer relied heavily upon imported American stars such as Paul Henreid, Tom Conway, Paulette Goddard, and George Brent among others, most of whose careers were already on the decline in Hollywood. But while the performers may have varied from film to film, the production units remained uniform. Hammer's staff and facilities were so limited only one production could be filmed at a time, resulting in a closely knit "family" type of organization of executives and technicians. The success of *The Curse of Frankenstein* brought the realization that major studio financing might soon be available, encouraging those involved to approach the filming of *Dracula* with an even greater degree of enthusiasm and care.

Overseeing the upcoming *Dracula*, as they had with *The Curse of Frankenstein*, were a trio of producers: Michael Carreras, Anthony Hinds and Anthony Nelson-Keys. Carreras had grown up within the company his grandfather Enrique Carreras co-founded with Will Hammer back in the mid-thirties. From 1943 until 1946, he gained experience in various departments eventually becoming a producer's assis-

Anthony Hinds

Peter Cushing with Anthony Nelson Keys

tant in late 1948. Following the death of his grandfather in 1950, Michael became a Director of Exclusive Films and worked on various films in the scripting, directing and producing capacities until 1855 when he was appointed executive producer of Hammer Films.

Of the over fifty films made by Hammer up until the time *Dracula* was released, nearly forty had been produced by Anthony Hinds. Hinds had entered the industry in 1939 as a booking-and -barring clerk with Exclusive and, following the war, became a producer for Exclusive in 1949, his first assignment being *Dr. Morelle — The Case of the Missing Heiress*. He served in the infrequent capacity of executive producer on Michael Carreras' first production *The Dark Light* (1951), but then reverted back to the role of producer, a position he held with Hammer throughout the decade into the sixties when he became actively involved in script writing under the pseudonym of John Elder.

Dracula's associate producer, Anthony Nelson-Keys (later simply Nelson Keys) was a seasoned veteran of more than one hundred British pictures prior to 1956. Entering the industry in 1928 he obtained experience in every technical department before the outbreak of the Second World War. Following that he worked as a production manager at Gainsborough Studios and on several color television productions. After serving as associate producer on several other British films (i.e. *Albert R.N., The Sea Shall Not Have Them, Reach for the Sky*, etc) he joined Hammer in 1956 as they were preparing *The Curse of Frankenstein*.

Michael Carreas

ers were undecided on whether to treat Sangster's script serious or tongue-in-cheek. Shortly before shooting commenced. Anthony Hinds, Peter Cushing and Fisher met to discuss the script and all agreed that it must be treated with complete integrity. It is interesting to speculate what the outcome of the film and Hammer's resulting "horror cycle" would have been been like had *The Curse of Frankenstein* been treated in a light-hearted fashion. Sangster's 1970 film, *The Horror of Frankenstein*, provides some indication of the type of film which Hammer might have produced in 1957 if an alternative approach had been taken.

Considering the family-type structure of Hammer, it was no surprise that the task of condensing *Dracula* into a form suitable for Hammer's budget (approximately 81,000 pounds or around $200,000 American Dollars at this timer) would fall to Jimmy Sangster.

All three producers unanimously agreed to the selection of Terence Fisher to direct *Dracula*. Fisher had slowly but steadfastly worked his way up within the film industry, first as a clapper boy (on *Falling for You,* 1933), then as an editor, eventually debuting as a director on the 1947 Highbury Production, *Colonel Bogey*. He had helmed eleven films for Exclusive/Hammer prior to *The Curse of Frankenstein* which he directed as he neared his fifty-fourth birthday. In retrospect, it is interesting to note how history might have been altered had it not been for a mishap and a series of coincidences. Fisher had originally been slated to direct and non-genre Hammer film, but the subject flopped midway through its production stage, leaving the studio owing Fisher not only money, but a film as well. At this point, as James Carreras sought to film a type of monster film which would elicit a degree of sympathy from its audience, Milton Subotsky (later co-founder of amicus Films) wrote a screenplay based on *Frankenstein*. Unable to secure financing for it, Subotsky allowed a friend to submit the script to Carreras. Whatever the reason(s) —the fact that it adhered rather closely to the novel may have made it financially impossible for Hammer to film it —Subotsky's screenplay was deemed unacceptable, and Jimmy Sangster was hired to write an original treatment. Sangster's script was accepted and he received sole screenplay credit for it, although Subotsky received a sum of money plus a percentage of the film's gross.[1]

With their facilities free for a few months, Hammer went ahead with plans to make their first *Frankenstein*. Initially unable to grasp its far reaching potential, the produc

Born in 1927, Sangster had joined Exclusive after the war serving as a second assistant director on one of the first "Dick Barton" films and becoming a production man

Jimmy Sangster

ager during the early fifties. In 1955 he was appointed assistant to Michael Carreras, and shortly after began writing his first scripts including *A Man on the Beach* (a 29-minute film of 1956), *X—The Unknown* (His first feature script and the last on which he served as production manager), and *The Curse of Frankenstein*. Hinds hired Sangster to adapt *Dracula* who, after reading the book for the first time, undertook the scripting during the late summer of 1957. completing his first draft in approximately four weeks time.

Dracula was slated to go before the cameras on November 4th, 1957, but due to normal production problems this was pushed back to November 11th with principal photography with the actors completed on Christmas Eve. The intervening time saw the sets for the upcoming film being designed, approved and finally constructed on the Hammer lot at Bray. Bray studios had been purchased by Exclusive at the onset of the fifties and remained Hammer's base of operations until 1967 by when they had outgrown its limited production facilities. Bray studios was situated on the banks of the River Thames just outside the village of Bray in Windsor. In 1949 Hammer had shifted their headquarters from nearby Cookham Dean to a large furnished manor house on an estate named Oakley Court just outside the village Bray. They filmed a few of their early productions in and around the Oakley Court house but were soon attracted to the possibilities the adjoining estate of Down Place offered. Although the owners of Down Place resided in a wing of their large manor house, the majority of rooms were either empty or being used for storage. During the shooting of *The Lady Craved Excitement* (1950), Hammer asked the owners of Down Place if they might shoot some sequences on their estate. Permission was secured and gradually everything shifted over to Down Place, with Hammer first renting, then buying the estate which became known as Bray Studios.

Although Bray would later expand to a greater number of sound stages, at the time *Dracula* was filmed there were but two stages and both of these adjoined the house. The first stage had once been the main downstairs room, an area of some eighty feet long by forty feet wide by fifteen feet high (after the ceilings were taken out). The second was a newly constructed brick state which served as the lab set for *The Curse of Frankenstein* before being struck in order to erect the "hall and stairway" set for *Dracula*. Down Place was a completely self-contained studio, with about four of its original bedrooms serving for sets, producer' offices and apartments, dressing rooms, a commissary, and even a projection theater all enclosed within its walls. The only exterior buildings were some little places erected to house a generator and to serve as a carpenter's shop. Strangely enough, the owners of Down place continued to reside in the wing of the house even after Hammer purchased the estate.

An invaluable member of the company's technical crew was its production designer, Bernard Robinson. Born in 1912, Robinson had been active in films from the mid-thirties although he did not join Hammer until June of 1956, immediately handling the sets for *X—The Unknown* and *The Curse of Frankenstein*. It was Robinson who conceived and supervised the design of countless Hammer sets from the mid-fifties up until about two years before his death in 1970, and deserves praise for the high standards of elegance achieved on the conservative funds afforded his department.

For *Dracula* the exterior castle set was extremely small in comparison to its appearance in the film. With relatively minimal funds at his disposal, Robinson designed and built an authentic looking medieval fortress. When Castle Dracula was introduced to audiences via a brief but imposing long shot, the exterior set was combined with an excellent glass painting giving the castle its high walls and turrets along with a distant background of snow-capped mountains. The illusion of foreboding majesty is most impressive.

For his interiors, Robinson's sets are notable for his twisted pillars and stained glass windows, but more than anything else, for his apparent zeal in cramming into his sets an abundance of antiques ranging from Victorian furnishings to an intricately carved chess set. These neve seemed out of place and gave the sets the superior look of a high budget production. Terence Fisher spoke highly of the sets saying, "They were a joy to work on because wherever you went on a Bernie Robinson set you could shoot with effect. There designed in such a way that no matter where you stood and looked you had interest."

While the sets were being designed and constructed, the cast selections were finalized. The combination of Peter Cushing and Christopher Lee had worked so well on the Frankenstein film that they were reunited, Cushing signed on to the project on October 9th, and Lee a few weeks later on October 29th. The studio's publicity department being quick to capitalize on the re-teaming of "Britain's Top Horror Stars" in many of the

Peter Cushing as Van Helsing in a scene from "Brides of Dracula" - the second Hammer Vampire film from 1960

Exisitng Castle before the matte painting was applied.

Melissa Stribling as Mina Holmwood

advance press releases. Michael Gough and John Van Eyssen were engaged for secondary male roles. Although Gough and achieved a certain notoriety the following decade for his portrayal of sadistic villains in second and third rate thrillers, he also managed to distinguish himself in major dramatic roles in important British television series and specials. He would later comment on his only Hammer horror film as one which "...didn't have imagination—the wild mountains weren't wild enough. I remember seeing Lugosi's Dracula and the bat flying around the coach where the drive should have been. The newer film lacked the atmosphere and the fantasy"[2] John Van Eyssen had been a minor character throughout the fifties, appearing in Hammer's *Four-Sided Triangle, Men of Sherwood Forest* and *Quatermass II (*Enemy from Space. Van Eyssen had spoken unflatteringly about both his early acting career and his films and has since gone on to become a high-ranking executive with Columbia Pictures.

For *Dracula*'s key female roles, the producers engaged Melissa Stribing, Carol Marsh, Valerie Gaunt and nine year old Janina Faye. Stribling had originally planned on becoming a film editor, but after meeting and marrying film director Basil Dearden turned her ambitions to the theater where she appeared in a number of stage and television productions including video adaptations of *Blythe Spirit* and *The Man in Half Moon Street*. She landed a key role in her husband's 1954 film, *Out of the clouds* and eventually retired from films in the sixties. Carol Marsh had also had a number of parts in several prior British films before being cast as Lucy in *Dracula*, including *Scrooge, Brighton Rock* and *Alice in Wonderland*. Valerie Gaunt's career in films was even more brief, with her roles in the first two color Hammer horror films her most memorable. Like Carol Marsh, she has since retired from films. Janina Fay's career was launched as a child actress in 1955 and she continued in the profession, appearing in several British television productions of the seventies. Her name was misspelled as Janine Fay on the closing credits of *Horror of Dracula*.

A few weeks before shooting began on *Dracula*, Sangster, Fisher and the three producers met to discuss the script. According to both Fisher and Sangster, these story conference were never very long nor involved, and Sangster could not recall doing any major revising after submitting his shooting script; his active participation on the production ended after his script had been approved, although he conceded that he "may have rewritten a scene or two."

Overall, Sangster's screenplay in an admirable job of screen writing, especially when one recalls it was written by a man who had only just begun writing for films. His script greatly modified and eliminated characters from the book, condensing the broadness of the novel in terms of time and place. Dracula's sea voyage to England and the character of Renfield (among other things) were deleted because, according to Sangster, "there just wasn't any room for them, although Thorley Walters did a Renfield-like character for *Dracula—Prince of Darkness.*" Although Hammer could not afford to convincingly have Dracula change into the form of a bat, Sangster stated that this was not the reason for its exclusion. "One of my reasons was that it had never been done very well and I tried to ground the script to some extent in reality. I thought that the idea of being able to

Janina Faye as Tanya

Carol Marsh as Lucy Holmwood - Arthur's sister

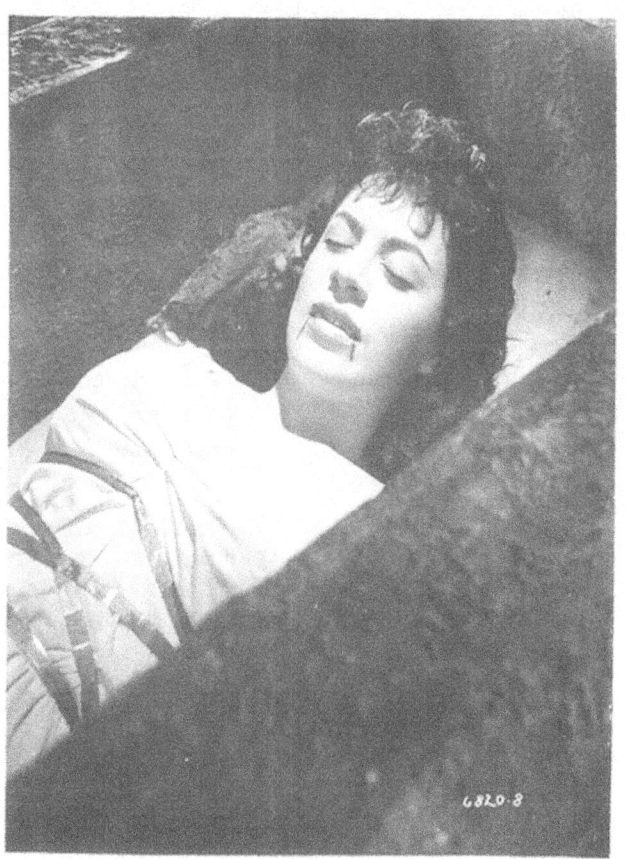

change into a bat or a wolf or anything like that made the film seem more like a fairy tale than it needed to be. And, fortunately, everybody agreed with me."

Following these story conferences, Fisher met with his cast to discuss characterizations, approach and wardrobe along with each member's own particular questions or problems. Cushing had read *Dracula* shortly after learning of his forthcoming role as Van Helsing and discovered that Stoker had described the vampire's nemesis as "a little old Dutchman with a bald head and sporting a small beard. All the production team got together and decided that it would be better to inject more vigour into the character, therefore I played the part more or less as myself. It would have been silly form myself to have been made up as a little old man...as they might as well have cast a little old man,"[3] Cushing's importance to the success of *Dracula* has usually been underrated, with Lee and Fisher receiving most of the accolades. In actuality, Cushing's contribution cannot be over exaggerated. Besides suggesting script alternatives which greatly enhanced key sequences, his Van Helsing was portrayed with such precision and vitality that it served as the perfect counter point to Lee's equally dynamic interpretation of Dracula.

Fisher had read *Dracula* many years before, finding it "heavy going" due to its structure (i.e. diaries and journals) and "It had not left any particular impression" upon him. He approached the adaptation with little more than a basic

Valerie Gaunt as the woman vampire asks John Van Eyssen (Jonathan Harker) for protection from Dracula.

knowledge of vampire legends and his own personal feelings regarding the vampires' sexuality which he later termed the 'attraction of evil." This feeling was one Fisher admits developed unconsciously as he began facing the task of "underlining what was already present in the script" during the filming of the picture. Fisher has termed himself "a working director," or one who will "see implications or what should be implications within a script."[4] The producers offered to screen the earlier versions of *Dracula* for Fisher but the director declined saying he did not wish to be influenced in any way by them. "Beyond consultation about the cast, the producers never bothered me. I didn't ask them for anything either. It turned out fine because it left me to direct the film as I wanted to."

Throughout *Dracula*'s twenty-five day shooting schedule Sangster's script underwent revision and tightening. Since Sangster has admitted to little if any participation on revising the script, it would appear that the changes were provided by Fisher with additional suggestions from his cast and Anthony Hinds. Although the shooting script dated "18.10.57" differs much from the final film, its structure remains basically the same. When broken down, the screenplay (and the film) consists of three stages.

I. Harker's arrival at Castle Dracula climaxing with his destruction and that of Dracula's mistress (thereby motivating Dracula's desire for revenge.

II. Dracula's revenge upon Harker's fiancee, Lucy Holmwood, and her subsequent release by Van Helsing.

III. Dracula's further attempts at revenge against Mina Holmwood concluding with her rescue and Dracula's own destruction.

In preparing the material for this article, I have had occasion to speak with Lee, Cushing, Fisher, Sangster and Carreras about *Dracula* and their involvement with it. Unfortunately, day-by-day details have become clouded by the passage of time and the information obtained was often confusing and sometimes contradictory. Having access to Christopher Lee's copy of Sangster's shooting script, I began to compare what was written with what appeared in the final print on the assumption that this would provide as close an analysis of how the production developed as it is presently possible to discern.

You can see how Sangster had conceived the film's opening sequence on page 41.

Fisher made only minor changes in this opening, such as beginning the sequence with an imposing closeup of one of the two stone eagles outside Castle Dracula. One of the major controversies surrounding *Dracula*, however, concerns whether or not the second sequence of Sangster's script—one in which we are introduced to Jonathan Harker—was actually filmed. The release print cuts from the dripping blood to several short shots of Harker approaching the Castle. Harker's voice is heard over these scenes, confessing his trepidation but indicating that he has a mission to perform. In contrast, for Sangster's original introduction to Harker see page 43-45.

In an interview with Gary R. Parfitt, Fisher denied that this coach sequence was films. There is enough evidence, however, to indicate that the scene was shot, though perhaps Fisher has forgotten about it. When reminded of the original opening Jimmy Sangster could not recall ever having written it. And, although Lee had crossed out scene six of this sequence in his script, the remaining scenes were left unmarked. *Dracula*'s British publicity folder, as well as Universal-International's New York office press sheet, credit the players involved and the roles they undertook. It is rather doubtful that these performers would have been credited anywhere had they not appeared in the film. In the one brief opening shot the film does afford us of the coach, it is manned by not only a driver but a companion as well, suggesting that the other players were also used.

Fisher's decision to edit this sequence out and replace it with a voice-over by Harker commenting on the time, place and mission (in such a way as to build curiosity concerning it) is far more original, expedient and less melodramatic handling of the sequence. Fisher's decision to cut the opening displays his intelligence in comprehending. Sangster's attempts at being much more subtle then previous versions in the events leading up to Dracula's appearance and also illustrates his ability to underline and develop these implications within the script.

Harker enters the castle to find himself in an elegantly if sparsely furnished main hall. A fire is blazing, an elaborate dinner has been laid out for him, and a note signed

Dracula leaves Harker unconscious and removes the vampire woman from the room–(To keep him for himself?)

"Dracula" invites him to eat well while apologizing for his absence. This note was signed "Count Dracula" in the script, but parentheses around the word "Count" by Lee in his copy indicate that the actor himself suggested its elimination. Although the setting would normally suggest an atmosphere of coziness and comfort, a sense of foreboding is felt by the audience, who is expecting something to occur at any moment. What occurs is the arrival of the vampire woman, sensuously portrayed by Valerie Gaunt, and the climatic introduction of Dracula.

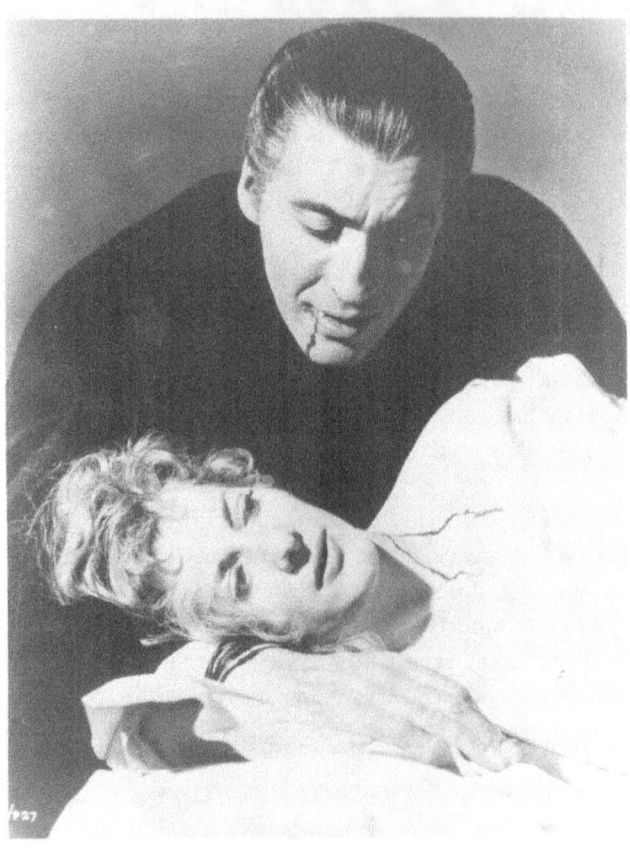

In the shooting script the vampire woman implores Harker to help her escape from the Castle and runs from the room as she senses Dracula's presence. Harker is swung around by Dracula's voice softly calling his name from a nearby doorway. Lee's handwritten notation on this scene — "Isn't it more effective to have presence bring J. round...no voice" —was a suggestion Fisher made use of combined with a dramatic positioning Dracula at the top of the stairs. The sequence from the script was later used in *Scars of Dracula* (1970) to much poorer effect.

Sangster described Dracula as:

"A tall man, his face is thin and saturine, with deep set eyes, high cheekbones, aquiline nose, high forehead topped by jet black hair.

When he speaks we may notice that his two canine teeth are slightly longer than normal, and definitely more pointed. One gets the impression that unless he makes a conscious effort to the contrary, these teeth would lay along his lower lip. As it is he keeps them well concealed, except when he talks.

He is wearing complete and unrelieved black, a costume cut in the severest lines. Over his suit he wears a long black cloak with a high pointed collar. He carries a black hat."

Once more some revision took place, this time in collaboration with hair stylist Henry Montash, makeup artist Phil Leakey, an costumer Molly Arbuthnot. Lee's makeup in his first scenes with Harker consisted almost entirely of a black wig of thick grey-streaked hair, brushed straight back in such a way as to provide an additional inch to Dracula's height and to give his facial features a decidedly satanic look. The hair also covered Lee's ear tips which suggested a certain wolfishness by creating an illusion that the vampires ears were pointed.

The "high-pointed collar" and "black hair" — identifiable with the Lugosi and Carradine interpretations—were ignored in favor of no hat and cloak whose wide spread collar reinforced the stream-line, cavalier characteristics of the Lee-Fisher-Sangster vision of Dracula. The lack of a crimson lining in the cloak—which Hammer later adapted for blood-red colorful effect - all the more stressed the somber, shadow-like substance of the vampire.

Fisher's handling of Dracula's introduction moves from climatic shock back to unnerving normalcy as Bernard's blaring three-note theme abruptly ceases to become immediately replaced by an ominous silence as Dracula rapidly descends the stairs to come into extreme closeup. This scene can be criticized because it allows Dracula's shadow to conspicuously appear against the wall to his side as he moves down the stairs but, in another respect, it is creative in that after the film was completed, all of Dracula's footfalls were erased from the soundtrack thereby developing a unique shadow-being or living shadow. Both Sangster and Fisher realized that audiences,, accustomed to Dracula films over the years, expecting a glaring, villainous figure; a youthful, virile Dracula is the first of Fisher's calculated attempts to begin building the suspense which would culminate with Dracula's demon-like entrance into the library. Fisher wisely avoided Sangster's suggestions in showing Dracula's canines which would only have diverted interest from the dialog—purposefully mild—as well as eliciting chuckles from those expecting to see something along those lines. Dracula's dialog is delivered at a clip and is concerned only with the comfort of his guest. A notable deletion from the shooting script were Dracula's lines:

"(Cont'd)....it is most unfortunate that I have to go again immediately. Your impression of me as a host must be abysmal, but what I must do is unavoidable."

Dracula's terming of his actions as "Unavoidable" lends support to Lee's often quoted comments about the "lone

HAMMER FILM PRODUCTIONS, LTD. Presents
"HORROR OF DRACULA"
Starring
PETER CUSHING • MICHAEL GOUGH • MELISSA STRIBLING and CHRISTOPHER LEE as Dracula
TECHNICOLOR *   A UNIVERSAL-INTERNATIONAL RELEASE

liness of evil" quality of Dracula, a characteristic which is difficult to perceive within Lee's initial performance as the vampire. "I've always tried to develop an element of sadness within the role. The character is not one to pity exactly, and the loneliness is expressed in an occasional way of saying something. It is not in the dialog itself and it's something which may not have come to me during the course of doing the first *Dracula*". However, although these remarks are generally attributed to interviews with Lee during the sixties, shortly after completing the film he was quoted in the British publication, *Picturegoer* (November 1, 1958 as saying," I tried to make Dracula a romantic and tragic figure. Someone you could feel sorry for." Sangster recently said, "In the first film we wanted to treat Dracula as the embodiment of evil with no redeeming qualities; I would say that he couldn't help what he was going but that didn't make him any less evil.... He enjoyed it....he also had a sort of revenge motive as he went for people who had destroyed his woman.

In spite of Sangster's statements, there are moments at the beginning of the film which do seem to mirror Dracula's loneliness. For example, Dracula's final words in the film, "Goodnight, Sleep well, Mr. Harker," are spoken in such a way as to hint at Dracula's cursed existence as being no longer able to have what he wishes his guest—a good night's rest. Lee has also said of his characterization, "I've always seen him as a very savage, sensuous person with a tremendous, primitive ferocity of blood; he had to be noble in his physical appearance and if he was going to be irresistible to woman, he had to be a superior being...strong."

In his shooting script, Lee questions Sangster emphasis on "Dracula's too perfect English & flawless grammar" terming it "slightly archaic." The actor realized that Sangster's dialog was British Victorian in style and that it would be possible—with his command of several languages—to instill within the character a suitably Central European accent. However, as play by Lee and the other cast members, the accents are entirely British although the story is set on the European continent. Many critics have

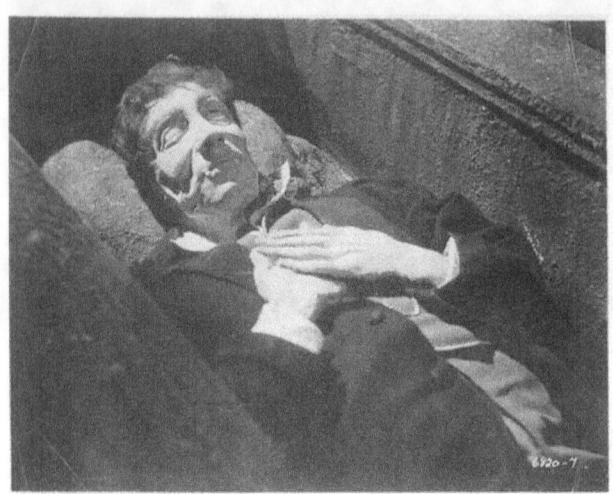
The vampiric remains of Jonathan Harker

stated their displeasure with the accents comparing them against the European accents and authentic Hungarian spoken by Lugosi and the villagers in the 1931 *Dracula*. Fisher answered these criticisms by saying, "We decided to play it without any foreign accents at all. Since the superstition is not a national superstition but a universal one it didn't need localizing. You aren't dealing with actuality but with a kind of fairy tale, and it isn't important to localize it. The other way of doing it is if you have an Englishman amongst a lot of foreigners with the foreigners all speaking marvelous English with a foreign accent, which if you analyses it, is equally silly." After their introductory remarks, Dracula picks up Jonathan's heavy suitcase with apparent ease and quickly moves towards the stairs, taking them two or three at a time, briefly explaining Harker's duties as a librarian while leading him to his room. In his script Lee noted, "point D's tremendous strength," in reference to Sangster's line. "But DRACULA takes it up as though it weighed nothing, swinging it in front of him as he moves up the stairs." After playing it as written, Fisher recalled that while viewing the daily rushes Lee began having second thoughts about the scene, believing it appeared sill what with Harker struggling to keep up with Dracula's movements, and suggested it be reshot or cut. Fisher disagreed, overruled him on the matter and the scene remained intact.

These dialog exchanges were purposely devised to portray Dracula as a polite and more human host, since audiences had long been accustomed to seeing Dracula in monstrous terms. Some of the dialog between Harker and Dracula was cut because it carried this politeness to an irritable extreme. Although he locks Harker's door (apparently to protect him from the vampire woman's advances), there is nothing in either Dracula's lines or manner which suggests that he has invited Harker to his home for any reason other than becoming his librarian. That such a monster would wish a "scholar to work among" his books is either the suggestion of a desire for human/intellectual compan

ionship to relieve his solitude or a simple plot contrivance indicating that Sangster was not concerned with this aspect of the characterization.

The action up until Harker's death was films much as written, except for the alterations made by Fisher as he blocked out each scene. Lee once called Fisher "very able...a fine arranger. He's a person who says, 'now, let me see what you're going to do,' and then steps in a molds it."[6] Examples of this molding can be found throughout this portion of the film, it was Fisher who wisely chose to have Harker see Dracula's dramatic and menacing stride from the Castle *after* making an entry in his diary about the vampire, rather than before the entry as indicated in the script. The director also modified Dracula's spectacular entrance into the library (referred to as a "Gothic room" in the script), opening the sequence with a shock closeup of Lee's blood-smeared face and having the actor leap over a book-laden table. A minor but interesting point about this sequence is the way that Dracula limits his actions against his guest, centering most of his fury on the vampire woman. Only when Harker persists in his attempts to stop Dracula does the vampire render him unconscious.

The character of Harker does not bear close scrutiny; his manner is simply too calm to be believed for a man who is aware of Dracula's true identity. That he accepts the vampire woman as a helpless innocent is a weakness of Sangster's script which can be overlooked because it is necessary to divert audience suspicion in order to build the explosive entrance of Dracula into the library.

Harker's actions when he regains consciousness are, however, utterly ridiculous. Although he must realize that he has precious little time in which to locate Dracula's tomb and destroy him. He wastes the precise amount of time he would have needed to make a final entry in his diary and to place it in the crotch of a tree just outside the castle. Harker then makes the mistake of dispatching the female vampire first before realizing that he should have destroyed Dracula. In all fairness however, such script ploys do work amazing wee in building and sustaining suspense. The audience has come to identify itself with Harker as the film's hero and therefore feels that he will not meet his demise so early in the film (a reprise later used in *Horror Hotel* and with greater success in *Psycho*).

Fisher chose not to follow Sangster's outline with the destruction of the vampire woman. Realizing that the film contained another such staking, the director decided to hold the explicit staking until second, a scene which required more excitement then the first. Instead he had the camera cut from Harker to his shadow at the moment he delivers the blow, then cutting back and forth between Harker and Dracula's face—at first shocked, then terrified, and at last confident of victory as he sees the last of the sun's rays fading. Only then does Fisher cut to what remains of the

Van Helsing explains to Arthur what must be done to free Lucy's soul

woman—a withered old crone. Fisher remembered that the extra who played the old woman was quite co-operative. "She suggested that she remove her false teeth to draw in her face. The only thing she didn't like, one little bit was getting into the coffin. She was very upset about that so I have her a kiss which reassured her it was all in fun; a sweet lady."

If any sequence within the film could be criticized for not improving upon Sangster's shooting script, is the original form Harker's death scene. As filmed, Harker discovers the empty sarcophagus and looks up to see Dracula entering the crypt from the outside slamming the door behind him. It is mystifying in that there is no apparent reason for Dracula to rise from his grave, leave the crypt, and then re-enter. Lee's memory of the sequence was hazy and he could only mistakenly recall that he was told to come through the doorway and that the camera did not cut to the door until he was standing in the entranceway. Sangster interpreted it "that he got out and came back purely for dramatic effect," then added, "In fact, the cut should have been to Dracula at the top of the steps just closing the door. In other words, he gone up the steps to close the door before coming back down."

Fisher chose to sum it up far differently by saying:

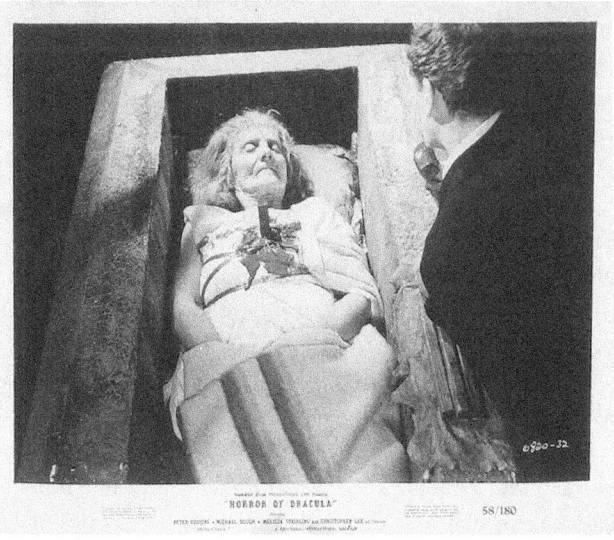

"Dracula did not wish to be in his grave anymore," and elaborated by commenting, "what I wanted to get at was the supernatural quality of Dracula, his power to overcome the limitation of time and space....his ability to walk through walls and to control or influence the minds of his proposed victims from a distance before actually appearing before them."

Following Harker's death the film dissolves to an epilogue which introduces the film's true hero—Doctor Van Helsing—and serves to illustrate what has happened to Harker. There seems to be a discrepancy in how Van Eyssen's appearance as a vampire was to be presented. Sangster described the vampiric Harker as: "Completely drained of all blood what is left merely skin over a skeleton. The skeleton hands are crossed in mock reverence over the chest, and the skull grins up at HELSING malevolently."

A dummy dressed in Harker's clothes and vaguely resembling Van Eyssen was designed for the production. Stills were taken of the "living skeleton" for publicity purposes, but it was never used. Fisher obviously felt that using Van Eyssen with a clip-on fangs was effective enough. Amusingly Hammer's budget was stretched so thing that Harker "inherited" Dracula's own sarcophagus upon Dracula's leaving the castle.

Following the epilogue of sorts, *Dracula* moves into its second stage in which society is characterized by the Holmwoods' life style and the relatively few people who come in contact with them because of Dracula. It is a society which is depicted a highly moral and orderly only to be temporarily thrown into a state of confusion and chaos by Dracula's debut within it. As in the novel, Dracula's appearances are considerably less frequent than in the beginning, with the completely eliminating the vampire's dialog as well. From this point on Dracula is presented solely as an exponent of evil and it is a credit to both writer and director that the film continually feels his presence throughout although the focus is shifted from Dracula to his victim (Lucy), her attempts to spread the disease (through Tania), and the contrasting schools of thought fighting to oppose this corruption (Seward vs. Van Helsing). As in the prior filmatic versions, Lee's Dracula symbolizes the very essence of evil. He is more than a sexual extension of the Lugosi Dracula for he embraces characteristics of Schreck's Orlok in that his Dracula also is the harbinger of death; the carrier of a vile pestilence which he brings forth from a remote corner of the globe to the supposed secure and sedate Victorian bedrooms of civilization.

Sangster's script also invested Dracula with the power to "stay buried as long as he wants to...years if necessary." It is only when Harker threatens his existence and destroys his woman that Dracula leaves his domain to revenge himself; a revenge specifically directed against the loved ones of the man who attacked him.

This revenge motif seems subjugated in interviews given by Fisher who has referred to *Dracula* as "nothing more, nothing less than a love story. [7] Asked to elaborate on this the director said, "It's an off-shoot of the love situation because Dracula has the power, in a twisted way, to make Lucy and Mina give a sexual reaction." And while Fisher merely sets the stage in the first reels for the eroticism to follow (i.e. Dracula's physical attractiveness; the buxom vampiress) he doesn't really begin emphasizing it until the second stage of the film.

Changes within the section were many, but minor. Sangster's script portrayed Arthur Holmwood as a much more violently tempered man, a characterization summarily watered down by deleting his lines emphasizing this, and by Gough's very sensitive and restrained performance. The drawing room sequence in which Van Helsing informs the Holmwoods of Jonathan's death is important for a number of reasons. It immediately reinforces the Victorian mood by the set, the costumes; and by the precise diction and polite mannerisms stressed by all parties. It also suggests that although the Holmwood residence is supposedly situated somewhere in Central Europe that it is England that Dracula has invaded. More than anything else, Fisher underlined and developed the elements and implications of sexuality and the decay of social mores which lay within Sangster's script.

Regarding these themes Fisher stated; "Both female characters in Dracula were so loosely written that it didn't mean a thing. I had to emphasize that these two women who were involved with Dracula were under a special influence. I thing what I dragged out from between the lines was a little more than possibly was ever implied within the script. That may be pompous, but I believe it's true." [8]

Fisher's feelings along these lines appear correct when comparing the film against the shooting script. Fisher's alterations in the sequence involving Dracula's nocturnal appearance at Lucy's bedroom and his subsequent sexual/vampiric attack upon her were interpretive changes. His approach to the sensual aspects of the scene made it almost lyrical, as if to suggest a bride trembling with anxiety and anticipation on her wedding night. "It's almost ballet the way she opens the doors, goes back and lies down again, her eyes focused, waiting for him to appear," Fisher mused. "You know, it's a distortion of the so-called true-love, and this is the power of evil working from a distance. Dracula could cause himself to appear there right at the moment when he realized that any resistance to him she might have had was gone."

One example of the numerous changes were the original lines preceding Dracula's closeup as he stands on the threshold of Lucy's room. Sangster had Van Helsing listening to his own voice on the primitive dictaphone stating:

(voice distort) Whose portrait was it? Was it that of Jonathon's fiancee, Lucy? If so why had Dracula taken it?....What could he have wanted with it

From these lines Sangster suggested a cut to Lucy's bedroom for a close shot of Lucy followed by a close shot of Dracula. Again Fisher strongly improved upon the

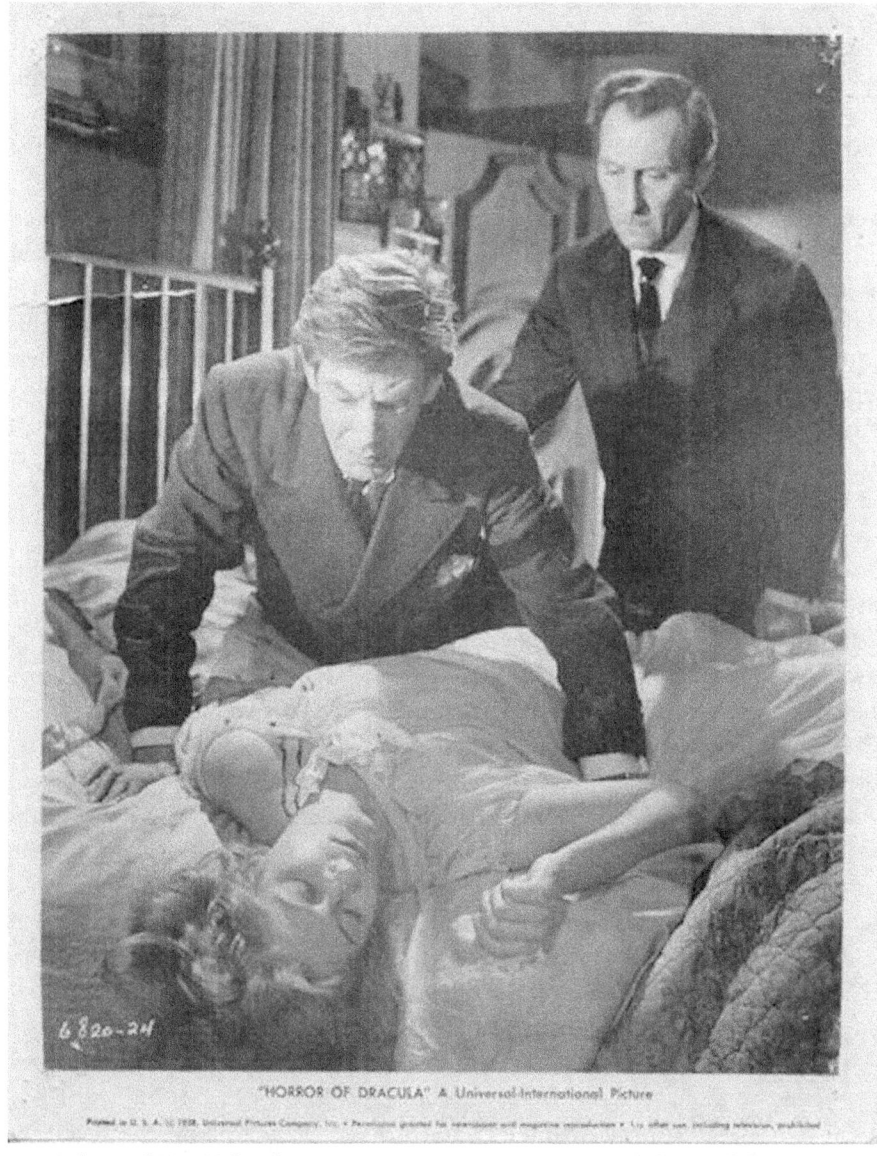

Arthur and Van Helsing's attempts to protect Mina from Dracula have failed!

original suggestion by having Van Helsing begin making a fresh dictaphone recording, which instead of questioning Dracula's obvious motives, imparts additional pertinent information:

> Established. That victims consciously detest being dominated by vampirism but are unable to relinquish the practice; similar to addiction to drugs. Ultimately death results from loss of blood but unlike normal death no peace manifest itself for they enter into the fearful state of the 'Undead.' Since the death of Jonathan Harker, Count Dracula, the propagator of this unspeakable evil, has disappeared. He must be found and destroyed!

Fisher then cuts immediately to an extreme closeup of Dracula's face, allowing the vampire to punctuate the scene by his mere abrupt appearance as he had previously done with the cut to him striding down the drive from his castle. The change in lines here is important, as it stresses the undercurrent of human corruptiveness associated with vampirism by drawing a parallel between vampires and drug addicts. This popular blending of excessive human plea sures with vampirism (signifying moral decay) would surface throughout Hammer's horror films, usually within the scripts written by Anthony Hinds under his pseudonym of John Elder. Since Sangster has admitted that he made few if any revisions upon his submitted shooting script, one might suspect that these additional lines and subthemes were contributed by producer Hinds who was actively involved in the creative end of Hammer's productions.

In the shooting script Van Helsing receives the blunt of Arthur's criticism for Lucy's death (Gerda does not step forward to admit her guilt because she is not present in the scene. The script also called for a funeral following Lucy's death in which Van Helsing hands Jonathan's diary to Arthur. Obviously, this was cut to expedite things, and the action was changed to having Van Helsing give the diary to Holmwood in his own house. Fisher eliminated more unnecessary dialog in the sequence in which Tania is questioned by the Holmwoods, Gerda, and the policeman about her whereabouts. Again the director wisely chose to climax upon Tania's revelation that her abductress was "Aunt Lucy," realizing that any additional exposition here (which

Sangster did add) would only be redundant and anti-climatic.

The script and film both cut to the scene involving Arthur's visit to Lucy's tomb. Although the actual staking is filmed as explicitly as Sangster wrote it, some changes leading up to this moment are worth noting. The script had Arthur arriving to discover Lucy's coffin (rather than open sarcophagus empty with the plate revealing her year of death as 1899 (fourteen years later than when the film itself takes place.

There is a cut to Gerda's room in the Holmwood house and a shot of Tania's empty bed (probably unfilmed as it would have called for the construction of another set for only a few seconds of film). Tania encounters Lucy within the woods having heard her "aunt" call her and Lucy leads the child off in the direction of the cemetery. Fisher chose not to insert a brief shot of a figure glimpsed only from the neck down but "wearing black clothes and a long cloak" since it made little sense to have Dracula appear if for such a minor reason as to watch the vampirizing of a little girl. Lucy leads the child to the graveyard and it is apparent that Tania has already been bitten since she complains of a "sore throat and because Lucy's shroud is bloodstained.

This was evidently not filmed because it might have been viewed as too severe to have suggested that the child was violated in any way. The scene in which Van Helsing suddenly appears to brand Lucy's forehead with his crucifix was left intact, but Fisher decided that it would be more convincing to let Van Helsing handle the staking rather than have Arthur strike the first two blows, and then, unable to continue, have Van Helsing finish the task. This might have increased the drama, but would have certainly drawn out the gruesome business. Fisher instead allowed the camera to cut to Holmwood painfully wincing at Lucy's agonizing screams. Although Sangster must be afforded the kudos or the criticism for devising the explicitly filmed staking of Lucy, both Fisher and Hammer have long been criticized for indulging too heavily in blood and gore for commercial purposes. Fisher retorted; "The critics who attacked me for being explicit never understood that what I wanted to show in the vampire films was the triumph of good resulting from the act of staking; that it was a release for the victim tainted with vampirism. I filmed the first staking in *Dracula* using shadows because it would have been far less exciting to have filmed them all the same way. But you can't show the destruction of the vampire solely by shadows or implications; you've got to be explicit since it is important that the release from vampirism be shown, just as it's important to show the resulting look of peace upon the victim's face.

With the destruction of Lucy Holmwood, *Dracula* enters its third and final stage. Unlike the transition between the first and second parts (which seemed to end one story before beginning another), the transition between the second and third stages is smoother if only because the major characters remain unchanged. Van Helsing and Holmwood decide to travel to the frontier station at Ingstadt to check on the final destination of Dracula's coffin. Arriving there, Fisher re-staged the confrontation between the frontier official (George Benson) and the two men. Originally, the scene was one which had the official steadfastly refusing to divulge any information until Van Helsing physically assaults him. Fisher decided to replace this violent outburst with a far more subtle and humorous device—having Holmwood bribe the man into talking. The director dramatically tied up this scene with the next one by having the official reveal the location of Dracula's coffin and then cutting to Mina standing in front of the address, another revision not in Sangster's script.

Following a brief shot of Dracula pushing back the lid to his coffin the film dissolves to the Holmwood sitting room the next morning. Fisher explained what occurred on the set at the time: "Dracula preyed upon the sexual frustrations of his women victims. The [Holmwood] marriage was one in which she was not sexually satisfied and that was her weakness as far as Dracula's approach to her was concerned. When she arrived back after having been away all night she said it all in one closeup at the door. She'd been done the whole night through, please! I remember Melissa saying, 'Terry how should I play the scene?' So I told her, 'Listen, you should imagine you have one whale of a sexual night, the one of your whole sexual experience. Give me that in your face!' And she did, of course. I have a blow-up, a closeup which I treasure. She was very good."

When Van Helsing and Holmwood visit mortician J. Marx, Fisher allowed character actor Miles Malleson to play the part to the fullest, telling a grim joke, chuckling, mumbling and slapping a coffin. Fisher spoke highly of Malleson calling him :a wonderful actor; you'd rehearse with him but you never quite knew how he would end up playing the scene since he was a great improvisor."

Dissolving from the mortician's shop back to the Holmwood residence that evening. Fisher continued tightening the script and as you will read, eliminated an interesting but unrelated little story delivered by Van Helsing.

The scene in which both men patrol the grounds about the house and Dracula's attack upon Mina is played almost exactly as conceived, including the shot of Dracula at the foot of the stairs and the shock cut to an owl hooting (an ironical use of the Lewtonesque "bus" insofar as it suggests nothing is amiss exactly as Dracula prepares to bite Mina. Dracula's sensuous actions were followed by Fisher and interpreted by Lee exactly as Sangster wrote them.

DRACULA takes MINA into his arms. She moans quietly. He gently brushes her forehead with his full lips...then her cheek...then her neck. MINA stops shuddering hold her breath. Then—

Van Helsing protects little Tania from furture attacks by "Aunt Lucy" whom Dracula has claimed as his first victim

"Dracula takees Mina into his arms. She moans quietly. He gently brushes her forehead with his full lips, then her cheek, then her nect. Mina stops shudering holds her breath. Then–" Jimmy Sangster

John Van Essyenn (Jonathan Harker - finds the mark of the girl vampire on his throat.

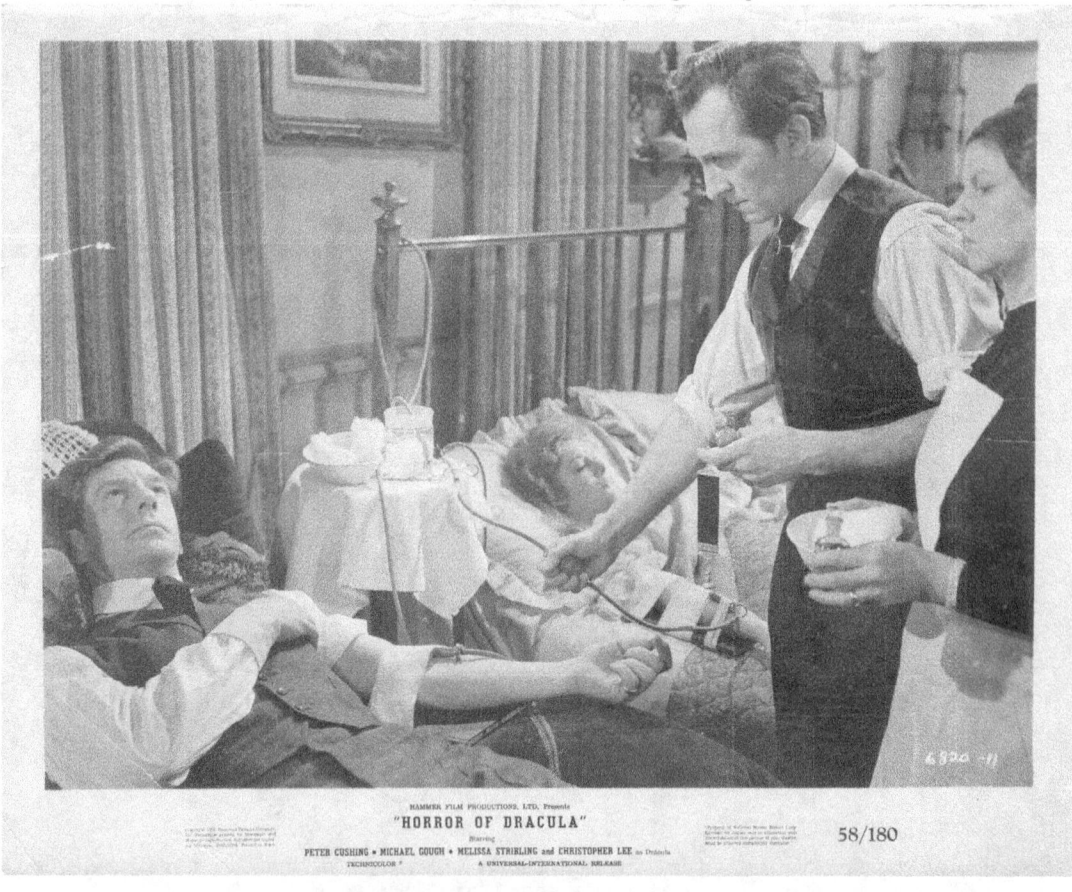

Gersa watches as Van Helsing gives Mina a trasfusion from Arthur after Dracula has attacted Mina

Arthur gives Mina a crucifix to protect her, unknowing that she has already become the victim of the vampire

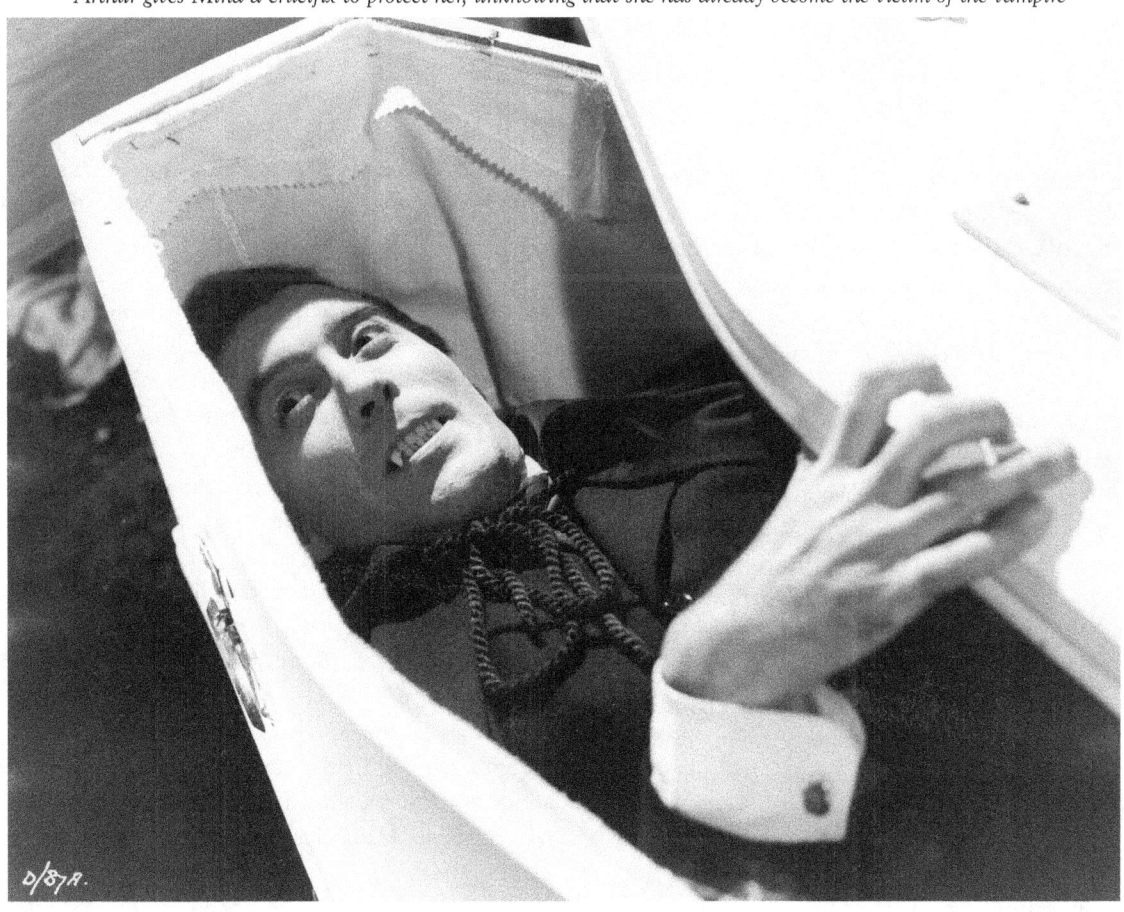
Dracula is in the house!

Gerta explains why she removed the garlic from Lucy's bedroom

Following Arthur's discovery of his wife and Van Helsing's primitive transfusion to save her life, key lines leading to the climax were significantly altered. The script found Gerda apologizing for bothering Van Helsing asking "... but have you any idea what Mrs. Holmwood wanted me to do with that box in the cellar?" This was revised to be less patiently revealing: "Well, sir, Madame told me the other day that I must on no account go down to the cellar." Van Helsing rushes to the cellar where he spies Dracula's coffin, discovers that it is empty as Dracula appears at the doorway for a moment before slamming and locking the door. Van Helsing leaves his crucifix in the box (preventing Dracula's return but leaving himself unprotected at the same time. His pounding and shouts bring Holmwood who frees him just as Gerda screams from the bedroom above them. Van Helsing's movements in this scene were directly attributable to Cushing who had asked Fisher if he might make a jump over the bannister instead of running around to the steps. The director replied that he shouldn't perform such a potentially dangerous stunt. However, when the scene was filmed, Cushing went ahead with the leap on his own accord and accomplished it perfectly in a single take.

Gerda's hysterical lines referring to Dracula as looking "like the devil" replaced some which stated in part, "his cloak flapped about him as he ran out like a giant bat." Fisher's next scene was a shot on a road with the two men discovering the mutilated body of a coachman (Dracula having stolen the coach to return to his castle).

Written but unfilmed was a short sequence involving a ruse by Dracula to get the coachman to stop by placing Mina's unconsciously body in the road, climaxing with a close shot of Dracula preparing to throttle the man.

The coach scenes were filmed just after down one morning on an almost deserted country road in the heart of Berkshire. Cushing, who refused to have a double for the scenes had been practicing the drive for two days and admitted at the time that he was having "enormous fun. It's something I've always wanted to do—and now I get paid for it, too."

Although the shooting script was followed in general, it remained for Fisher and composer Bernard to instill within the climax the superb blend of pacing and action which has made it a classic and the most memorable of all of Hammer's finales.

Had the shooting script been filmed as written the cli-

matic confrontation between Dracula and Van Helsing-would have been dramatically inferior. The scene in which Dracula hurls Mina into an open grave was faithfully filmed although two takes were required. On the first, as Lee was about to hurl Melissa Stribling's double into the hole, he stood too near the edge, lost his footing, and fell in on top of her! The elimination of Dracula's footfalls from the soundtrack as he rushes into his castle, through its halls, and up the stairs to the library was one additional afterthought but the dynamics of the ensuing battle should mostly be credited to Fisher and Cushing. Realizing that the shooting script had Dracula being destroyed almost solely by his own actions, Fisher reblocked the scene so that it contained a physical struggle between the two in which Van Helsing's wits were played against the vampire's own cunning and strength. Van Helsing quickly masters the situation by tearing the draperies from the windows flooding the room with sunlight. Since the set differed from Sangster's vision of it, Fisher was again presented with a set which suggested alternative possibilities for blocking the scene. As in Dracula's earlier fight with Harker, the long table upon which several stacks of books lay scattered about became a prop of key importance. Cushing felt that the climax would be immensely improved if it were possible for him to leap from a balcony upon the draperies, pulling them to the floor. As the set lacked a balcony, the table served the same purpose. Cushing's double (the only time in the film when the actor required a stunt man) jumped

on the table then ran along it to the end, leaping to the windows. Cushing's familiarity with a Shakespearian play inspired him to devise his following course of action, that of seizing up the two candlesticks from the table and forming a cross which forced Dracula to fall back into the fatal pool of light. Fisher filmed all of the closeups of both actor's reactions including a shot in which Lee's hand tore at his partially disintegrated face, which was edited out of the British and American prints bet remained in the French and Japanese.

The climax of *Dracula* was filmed during the productions final shooting day. Hinds kept pushing the crew to finish up so that the sets could be struck for the next production. Although Fisher admits that he and Robinson had adapted themselves to the pressures that time and budget inflicted upon them, his lighting cameraman, Jack Asher, "probably felt the pressure more than Bernie or I because Jack hated to compromise. I would have liked to spend a little more time on rehearsal but you'd have your target for the day and had to watch the clock. Jack found that very difficult because he was a great idealist ...a superb cameraman." Art professor and film critic David Soren beautifully characterized Asher's photography on *Dracula* when he wrote:

London premier at the Gaumont Theatre

"Eschewing the traditional Stimmung (atmosphere) of Universal (the remnants of German expressionism and the haze and fog, he used color to evoke mood. In *Horror of Dracula* red is the Leitmotiv which signals the presence or influence of *Dracula: the* red blood on his lips, the red curtains in the houses. And not just red, but RED—deep and intense. The red is kept in careful contrast to the cold colors of death, the pale grey and blue of a corpse in the sepulchre of Dracula. Red and blue colors hover menacingly about Miss Lucy and produce a subliminal malaise in the careful viewer." [10]

Two or three weeks of additional post-production work followed, with Sidney Pearson and his special effects crew filming the decomposition closeups of Dracula's disintegrating limbs and head.

Perhaps coincidentally, Hammer chose to promote their *Dracula* much the same way as Universal had promoted their version in 1931. The Lugosi film was touted as being "The story of the strangest Passion the world has ever known!" while Hammer modernized their basic campaign around "The TERRIFYING Love—who died—yet lived!" and "Who will be his Bride ... tonight? Hammer's publicity department developed the usual number of wide-ranging press releases. One of these concerned the visit to the set of *Dracula* by Bram Stoker's great-grandson, twelve year-old Robin, who was quoted as predicting, "When I grow up I'm going to be an actor like Mr. Lee and terrify people by playing Dracula myself" The truth may have undergone some stretching by quoting that the three femme stars of the film were too frightened to see the picture. Another highly improbable press release was:

"Melissa Stribing ... has an odd off-set play-pastime. A brilliant archer, she could sometimes be found after lunch shooting apples off her stand-in's head with a bow and arrow! It's enough to make the average stand-in sit this one out, but pretty Daphne Baker didn't mind. She must have nerves of bitumenised steel."

But perhaps the most amusing story concocted by Hammer's publicity people was this one:

"Christopher Lee ... has been having a rough time finding an apartment ... Practical jokers at his last address were in the habit of leaving a saucer of blood on the door step with the early morning milk bottles. His landlady objected! So Chris is on the move..."

Dracula was completed in April of 1958 and rushed into release almost immediately. Hammer had previously concluded contracts which called for the film to be released domestically by Rank and world-wide by Universal-International (who also received credit for "presenting" the film in Great Britain). The film had a May 2nd press screening in New York City where U-I had already decided to alter its title to *Horror of Dracula*, thus distinguishing it from the often reissued and familiar Lugosi classic while emphasizing and capitalizing on the new films more lurid aspects.

Among the first critics to review the film was Variety's "Gilg" who predicted the production "should pay off handsomely at the b.o. despite the non-name cast," while going on to praise the film on all levels. Other trade papers were similarly in accord. *Box Office* terming it a "top notch horror drams" while the *Hollywood Reporter* said, "A lavishly mounted impressive production. Excitement and intrigue permeate the film." *Harrison's Reports* went so far as to say, "Tops them all ... It's shock impact is so great that it may well be considered as one of the best horror films ever made."
Following a May 2nd New York press screening *Horror of Dracula* had its world premier at the Warner Theater in Milwaukee, Wisconsin, on May 8th. According to *The Motion Picture Daily* the film rolled up an impressive first day's gross of $1,682 going on to top "all previous Universal pictures to play the house in the past four years," by attaining a total of $10,600 during its first five days. Universal supported the film in most situations wit their own latest state-side production *The Thing That Couldn't Die*. Key city openings in Detroit and Chicago followed immediately thereafter with the picture(s) doing smash business everywhere.

The film's producers and stars were on hand for the gala London premier at the Gaumont Theatre on May 20, and engagement which went all out in publicizing the event by huge poster and photographic displays. *Variety* reported that the film garnered about $13,000 during its first week.

While the critic for the prestigious London *Times* complemented Sangster's screenplay for retaining "something of the precise formality of the Victorian dialogue," he seemed to brush the picture off as "a horrific film, and sometimes a crude film but by no means an unimpressive piece of melodramatic story-telling." The critics for the *Daily Worker* and the *Observer* were somewhat less charitable, the former condemning the film as one which "disgusts the mind an repels the senses, while the latter saw fit to extend apologies to the American populace for 'sending them a work in such sickening bad taste." Perhaps the most negative of all came from film critic Peter John Dyer. Dyer, who simultaneously had his "Some Nights of Horror" essay on classic fantasy films published in the July issue of *Films and Filming,* obviously disliked Hammer's overall style in general. His review of *Dracula* began: There are boring horror films, and tasteless horror films. This new version of *Dracula* is a boring tasteless horror film." He went on to criticize the Hammer version for not following the Lugosi film and concluded with a comment on what he felt was an over abundance of blood—"Blood dripping on Dracula's coffin, trickling down his chin, streaming over Mina's nightie, you get it all over your and and you neck and your teeth, and it's pumped into you and out of you, an no wonder the makeup man's name is Phil Leakey."

But Hammer had experienced this same kind of negative criticism towards their approach with *The Curse of Frankenstein*, were prepared for it, and not unduly concerned with it. In most cases the adverse criticism was as effective as the raves in sending patrons into the theaters. Commenting on the productions, Anthony Hinds defended Hammer in a pre-release press notice entitled "Horror is My Business!" in part, he said:

"On T.V. programmes, in newspaper interviews, and even in my tavern, people always ask the same question: 'Why do you make pictures like *Frankenstein* and *Dracula*? And my reply is always the same: 'For the same reason you do your job—to make money.'

But, really, there's more to it than that. I find turning into a film a script loaded with opportunities to make ordinary people shudder and scream is also fascinating and fun.

I've been written of as a monster, a ghoul who exploits the barest, most degraded tastes in human nature for personal profit.

I can deny that simply by saying we don't drive the public into the auditorium to see horror on their screens. They go because they want to. They go because horror—the search for it, the experience of it, and also the enjoyment of it—is an even more fundamental human quality that the profit motive.

And, in my opinion, it's a healthy quality when it's harmless and harnessed—in a cinema.

Again, I am accused of introducing an UNNECESSARY degree of horror into my pictures. Now, this needs some sort of explanation, if only to justify myself as a film-maker with a conscience.

It is my job to make films as horrific as I can make them just as I would turn out funny films as funny as I could make them if I were in the comedy business.

We have observed that the age of the mechanical monster, the drudity of the unbelievable, is over. Today, a monster must be as acceptable—to the imagination, that is—as the man sitting next to you in a bus. We have to persuade the filmgoer, while he's in the cinema at any rate, that he is seeing reality on the screen.

That's why in *Dracula,* which we are making in colour, the title player Christopher Lee, looks almost normal. That is the secret of successful horror film-making—it is almost possible, it could happen to you!

So we set out to make *Dracula* into a man whose actions and appearance were always credible—even to the
 last horrifying scene. The horror is very nearly tangible—because it could be true."

Christopher Lee, Peter Cushing, James Carreras and Anthony Hinds arrive in New York City for the premiere

James Carreras, Hinds, Lee and Cushing flew to the United States following the gala May 22nd British premier at the Gaumont, Haymarket Theatre (Where it would go on to break house records) to participate in the New York City premier at the Mayfair Theater. Having received an abundance of laudatory notices as well as high grosses, Universal expanded their initial plans of holding an all night horrorthon on Tuesday, May 27th, to include the 29th and 30th as well. Some of the macabre touches accompanying the midnight premier were "courage cocktails" and an opportunity for the audience to file their last will and testament before seeing the picture (an idea possibly inspired by a similar William Castle gimmick for his recently released *Macabre*) Stars from the Broadway ligitimate shows joined the British celebrities and the festivities were covered on the city's WOR Long John Nebel midnight to six a.m. radio program.

The New York City daily papers carried impressively designed ads on the film's opening days making extensive use of trade paper quotes while ballhooing the availability of both Lee and Cushing for autographs during the May 28th eleven-thirty a.m. and seven-forty-five p.m. performances. Since Hitchcock's *Virtigo* opened the same day, the task of reviewing *Horror of Dracula* for *The New York Times* fell to the paper's junior critic. A.H. Weiler, who promptly displayed his ignorance when he served the film a luke-warm notice commenting that "there are strong indictions that the once gory plot is showing definite signs of anemia."

Horror of Dracula (sans *The Thing that Couldn't Die*) played three weeks at the Mayfair, Variety reporting totals of $25,000 for its first week followed by receipts of $17,000 and $14,000 respectively. The Hammer film outgrossed other current film fare such as *Cowboy* and *God's Little Acre* in the city and, considering its budget and "non-name" cast, did commendably well against the Hitchcock film which for the same three weeks registered $46,000, $39,000, and $28,000 (much of the difference here was also due to the varying ticket prices—$1.70 for *Dracula;* $2.50 for *Vertigo*)

With Famous Monsters of Filmland still in its infancy, there were no film fanzines to reflect upon "fan" reactions of the time. However, William C. Thomaier (a pseudonym for editor-publisher Calvin T. Beck) wrote in the first and only issue of *The Journal of Frankenstein* that the film lacked "great atmosphere" and a "baroque buildup" but conceded that the film began "jumping when, in color, the blood begins to flow."

Dracula proved to be an even greater shot in the arm for Christopher Lee's career, the actor noting this name now meant more in the United States than "Bogarde, Mills or Hawkins put together." [11] He almost instantly became something of a heart-throb to girls and women, much like Lugosi had become after playing Dracula. "I'm frankly puzzled," admitted lee. "An odd sex manifestation...Maybe it's because I tried to make Dracula a romantic and tragic figure. Someone you could feel sorry for," It's interesting to note that Lee could not grasp Dracula's significance as a Victorian sexual liberator which probably accounted for the reaction from females the world over. While he continued acting for Hammer (generally in supporting roles, it was not until 1965 with the filming of both *Dracula—Prince of Darkness* and *Rasputin—The Mad Monk* that Lee's career began soaring to high levels.

The Motion Picture Daily announced shortly after *Horror of Dracula*'s release that Hammer and Seven Arts Productions had entered into a multiple picture deal with Universal-International which included a sequel to *Dracula* to be produced "on the same large scale." For whatever the reasons, the sequel never emerged until years later when *The Revenge of Dracula* screenplay by John Sansom (Jimmy Sangster) was filmed and released as *Dracula—Prince of Darkness. Dracula II* was filmed in 1960 but Lee was not approached to appear in what was ultimately released as *The Brides of Dracula.* Warner Brothers-Seven Arts obtained the release rights to *Horror of Dracula* in 1964 and reissued it on a double bill with *The Curse of Frankenstein.* So popular was this combination with the drive-in circuits that the films continued to be paired together in theatrical playdates even during the seventies, although *Horror of Dracula* has been sold to American television in 1968. While it escaped the ignominious fate of *The Kiss of the Vampire* (retitled and butchered by television censorship) some small cuts were inflicted upon television prints of *Horror of Dracula*. Carol Marsh's first ear-shattering scream when being staked was cut (it being too loud for late night viewing) as were some of the more explicit shots of the staking by some local stations. Had the CBS network obtained the video rights to the film it might not have escaped the censor's shears so easily. During the CBS late night premier of *Dracula—Prince of Darkness*, closeups of Lee disintegrating body (during the introductory footage lifted from the climax of *Horror of Dracula*), were almost entirely deleted.

For a genre film buff such as myself who fondly recalls that August 16th Saturday matinee screening at the Capitol Theater in Whitehall, New York (perhaps appropriately enough, two years to the day of Bela Lugosi's death) it seems difficult to imagine that fifty-five years have passed since the release of *Horror of Dracula*. Time has often dealt harsh blows to the horror films of yesterday, emphasizing primitive techniques and overly melodramatic thesping, turning classic horror into contemporary comedy. Since Hammer inaugurated their horror cycle they have continually strived to develope their various themes, but most of these attempts have invariably failed to do anything but call up memories of their initial triumphs. Hammer's emphasis upon blood and gore (relatively mild when compared to today's films) gradually increased until the explicitness no longer became justified or controlled, but simply disgusting (i.e. the regurgitating of Dracula's blood by Ralph Bates in *Taste the Blood of Dracula*). Eroticism, within Hammer's films continued unabated with perhaps the peak of its tasteful application being Don Sharps's *The Kiss of the Vampire*. With the relaxing of the censorship code, nudity became the next logical step, so brief sequences were inserted in the company's *Carmilla*-inspired trilogy of the early seventies (i.e. *The Vampire Lovers; Lust for a vampire; Twins of Evil*). But in most instances the nudity accompanied scenes which were contrived (Ingrid Pitt chasing Madeleine Smith about a bedroom in *The Vampire Lovers*) or simply sickening ridiculous (the love making sequence from *Lust for a Vampire* with the song "Strange Love" grinding away on the soundtrack). Hammer ultimately felt they could revitalize the vampire film by distorting common legends and adding the element of swashbuckling (i.e. *Captain Kronos—Vampire Hunter*), but unfortunately none of the players could wear a cloak like Lee or deliver a line like Cushing. Sensing there was no limit to the number of Dracula and Frankenstein films that could be produced for a horror-hungry public, Hammer began (in Lee's words) "churning out Dracula and Frankenstein films like a sausage machine." The result was that Hammer and their distributors had misread the market. Warner Brothers took a loss on *Dracula A.D. 1972* during its highly publicized New York City run, and chose to take tax write-offs on their next two Hammer acquisitions—*The Satanic Rites of Dracula* and *The Legend of the 7 Golden Vampires*. The seventies saw the emergence of the big-budgeted horror films with the release of both *The Exorcist* and *Jaws*. If nothing else, these films served to place the hitherto respected "high quality" characteristics of the Hammer productions in a more proper perspective.

But by its realistic approach to its supernatural theme and by carefully underplaying rather than overplaying, *Horror of Dracula* has succeeded in transcending the decades. For its inspired casting of Lee and Cushing, its carefully calculated shocks, and its sustained pacing and suspense it remains as fresh and exciting as anything currently being produced. By possessing superior qualities in terms of script, photography, and set design it has escaped from being identified with such "cult classics" as *Carnival of Souls* and *Night of the Living Dead*, while continually being regarded as a lavishly mounted production. Considering its $200,000 production cost and noting that this amount was substantially less than it took to film a picture such as *Hillbillys in a Haunted House* (a 1967 film budgeted at $240,000[12]) while hardly denting the cost for the special effects of either *The Exorcist* or *Jaws*, *Horror of Dracula* emerges as a spectacular triumph of filmaking and a film which fully deserves its reputation as a modern classic of its genre.

Christopher Lee and Peter Cushing signing autographs at the Premiere

FOOTNOTES

[1] Milton Subotsky, "Milton Subotsky," *Little Shoppe of Horrors*, March, 1973, p.24 Interview by Richard Klemensen.

[2] Michael Gough, "The Incomparable Michael Gough," *Fantastic Worlds*, Number Two, 1972, p.29. Interview by David Soren.

[3] Peter Cushing, *The Films of Peter Cushing*, 1975, p. 29. Interview by Gary R. Parfitt.

[4] Terence Fisher, "Terence fisher: Underlining," *Cinefastastique*, Fall 1975, p. 24. Interview by Harry Ringel.

[5] Antohony Hinds, "Following the Footsteps of Dracula," *Fandom's Film Gallery*, Number One, 1975, p. 23. Interview by Sam L. Irvin, Jr.

[6] *Christopher lee*, "Interview with Chris Lee," *Castle of Frankenstein*, Number Twelve, p.45.

[7] Fisher, Terence Fisher: Underlining," p. 9

[8] *Ibid.*, p. 26

[9] Peter Cushing, "Peter Cushing's Coach and Pair," "Dracula" *Publicity folder*, 1958.

[10] David Soren, "Blood, Cleavage and Art, *Fandom's Film Gallery*, Number one, 1975, p. 45.

[11] Christopher Lee, "Chillers A Menace" Rubbish Says Christopher Lee," *Picturegoer*, November 1, 1958, p.5

[12] Michael B. Druxman, *Basil Rathbone* (Cranbury, New Jersey: A.S. Barnes and Co., Inc., 1975) p. 357

ACKNOWLEDGEMENTS:

I wish to thank Christopher Lee, Jimmy Sangster, and Terence Fisher for their individual kindnesses in permitting themselves to be interviewed at length. All unfootnoted quotations by these gentlemen appearing in the article are from my own interviews with them. The Lee interview was conducted in August, 1970; the Sangster interview during August, 1976; and the Fisher interview(s) during May-June, 1976. I further wish to express my gratitude to Tise Vahimagi, for conducting the Fisher interview on my behalf and for pertaining additional background information; to Bob Sheridan who shared some additional information with me from his own interview with Fisher; and to Richard Klemensen who generously provided some of the stills used in this book. - Ronald V Borst

HORROR OF DRACULA
(British) Hammer Films, 1958

82 minutes; 7332 feet; Eastman Color Processed by Technicolor; Released in the U.S. by Universal-International on May 8, 1958 (world premier); Released in Great Britain by Rank as *Dracula* on May 22, 1958; Released in France as *Le Cauchemar de Dracula* by U-I on February 4, 1959; Executive Producer-Michael Carreras; Produced by Anthony Hinds; Associate Producer-Anthony Nelson-Keys; Directed by Terence Fisher; Screenplay by Jimmy Sangster; Based on the novel *Dracula* by Bram Stoker; Director of Photography - Jack Asher, B.S.C.; Production Designer-Bernard Robinson; Music Composed by James Bernard; Music Conducted by John Hollingsworth; Production Manager-Donald Weeks; Special Effects-Sidney Pearson; Supervising Editor-James Needs; Edited by Bill Lenny; Assistant Director-Robert Lynn; Camera Operator-Len Harris; Makeup by Phil Leakey; Makeup Assistant-Roy Ashton, Sound Recordist -Jock May; Costumes by Molly Arbuthnot; Hair Stylist-Henry Montasash: Continuity-Doreen Dearnaley; Stills Cameraman-Tom Edwards; Filmed at Bray Studios, England.

Cast: Peter Cushing (Doctor Van Helsing, Christopher Lee (Count Dracula), Michael Gough (Arthur Holmwood), Mellissa Stribing (Mina Holmwood), Carol Marsh (Lucy Holmwood), John Van Eyssen (Jonathan Harker), Olga Dickie (Gerda), Valerie Gaunt (Vampire Woman). Janina Faye (Tania), Barbara Archer (Inga), Charles Lloyd Pack (Doctor Seward) ,George Merritt (Policeman), George Woodbridge (Landlord), George Benson (Frontier Official, Miles Malleson (J. Marx, the Undertaker), Geoffrey Bayldon (Porter), Paul Cole (Lad). Guy Mills (Coach Driver), Dick Morgan (Driver's Companion, John Mossman (Hearse Driver), and in deleted scenes: Judith Nelmes (Woman in Coach), Stedwell Fulcher (Man in Coach), Humphrey Kent (Fat Merchant, William Sherwood (Priest).

Mina and Arthur see the mark of the vampire on her palm has vanished with Dracula's destruction by Van Helsing

BEHIND THE SCENES

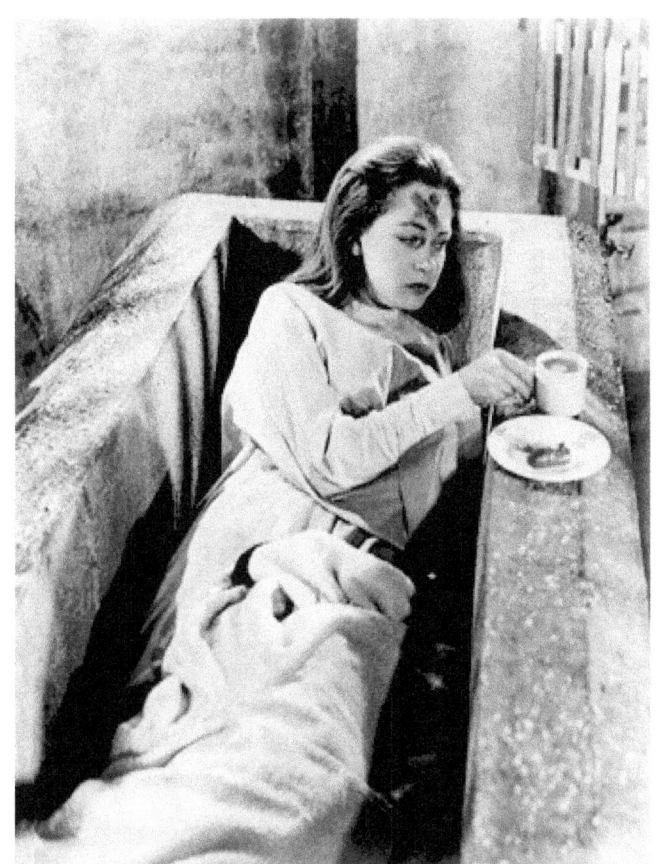
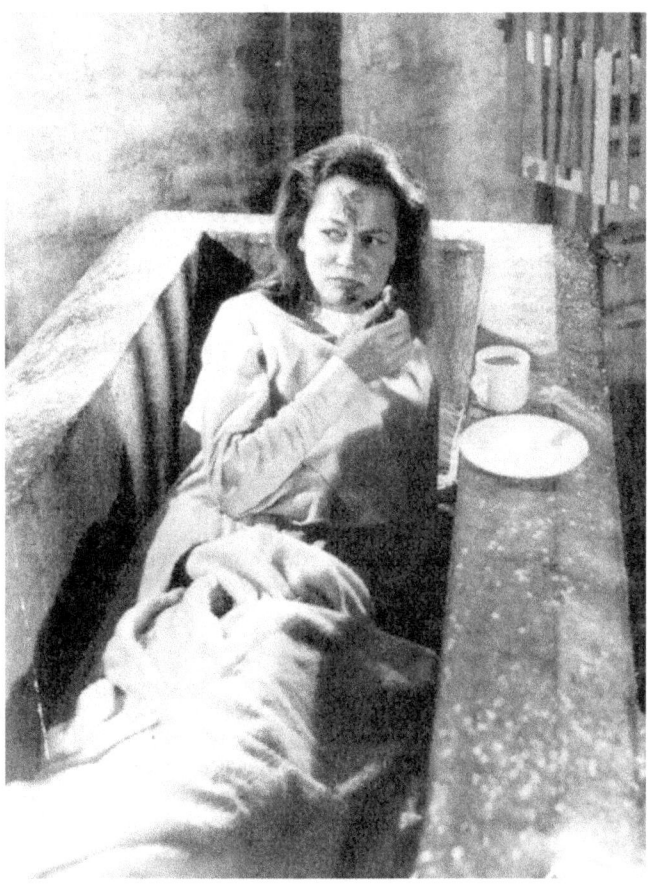

Terence Fisher with Christopher Lee

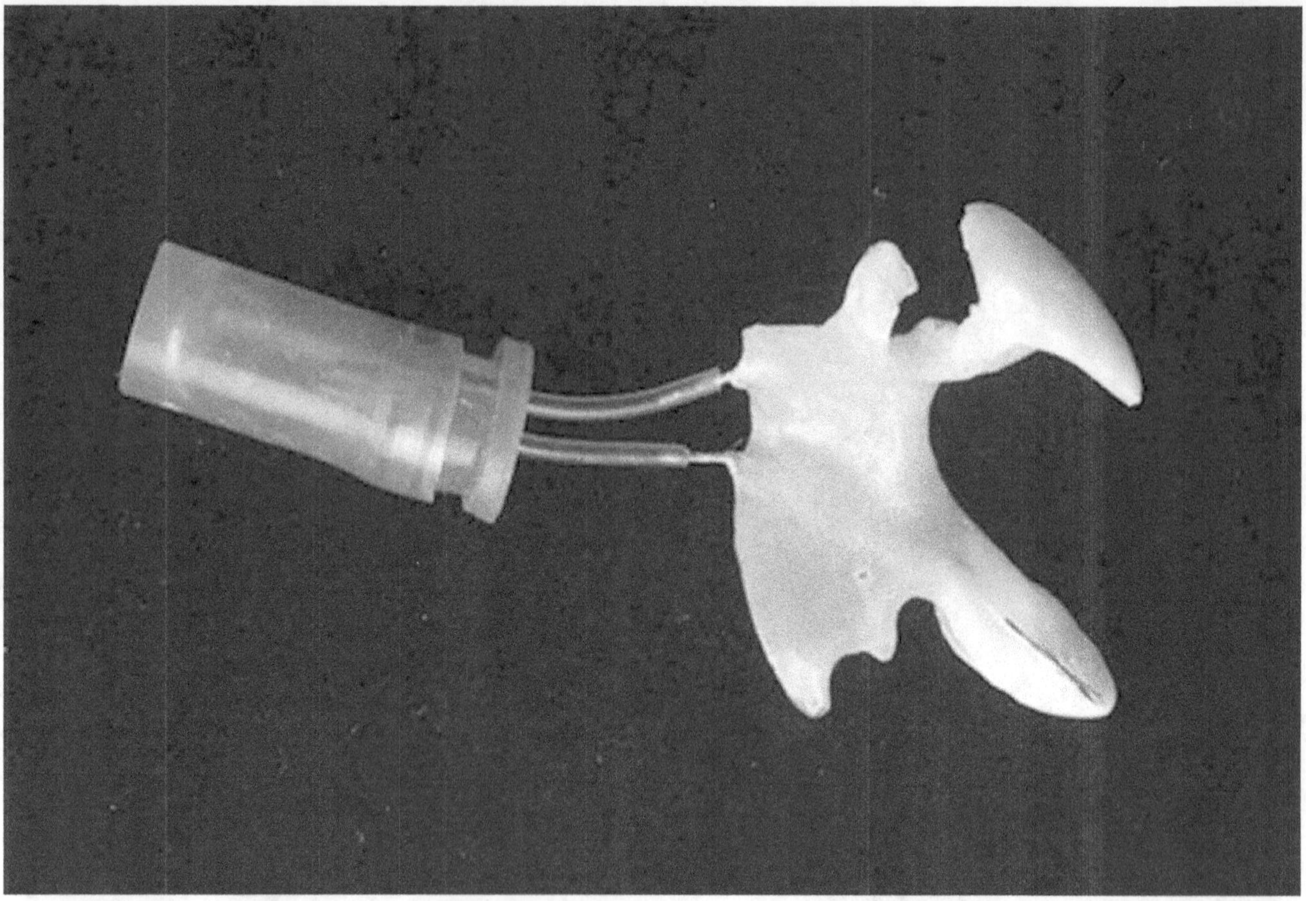

The fangs were created by Hammer make-up artist Phil Leaky and operated by Christopher Lee's tongue activating the blood chamber.

(Above the art department's drawing of Lucy's tomb set - (Below) the actual set

Set stills of the "sitting room" above - below Arthur's bedroom.

Set Designer's sketch on Castle Dracula's main hall - below the exterior set of the castle entrance.

English 1958 One Sheet - Courtesy of Richard A. Ekstedt

1. EXT. DRACULA MAUSOLEUM. LOT. DAY

We open on a late afternoon sky. A sky heavy with menace, with angry clouds shouldering their way across one another, completely shrouding the sun.

It is a scene in black and white, without any concession to colour whatsoever, just the graduations of grey black, black grey.

Over this we fade in all titles:

As the last Credit fades CAMERA pans down to disclose the mausoleum.

It is large, weather beaten, and eaten with age.

CAMERA passes the edge of the roof and on down to the door, which stands open.

CAMERA starts to track towards and through the open door.

Still we have seen no colour, everything being toned to the monotony of Black and White.

CAMERA tracks through to....

DISSOLVE:

2. INT. DRACULA MAUSOLEUM. STUDIO. DAY

Inside the mausoleum we still held the monotony of shading.

Here all is deathly quiet and still. There are two coffins set on plinths in the centre of the mausoleum, one slightly more ornate than the other.

It is towards the grander of the two that the CAMERA moves.

Then when it centres this coffin to the exclusion of the other we see carved in the side of the plinth one single word.

It is carved deep as though to last for all time.

DRACULA

We hold the carving for a long moment as the music builds and builds. Then silence........and from out of frame there drops into picture a vivid scarlet splash.

It is blood. It splashes across the carving on the plinth, forms small rivulets, and starts to trickle down the side of the plinth as we:

FADE OUT:

(1 - 2)

FADE IN:

3. EXT. COUNTRY ROAD. LOCATION. DAY.

This is a country road lined with trees, forming almost a tunnel through the forest.

Although it is late afternoon, and an occasional glimpse of the sky shows this, here beneath the trees it is almost as dark as night.

We are shooting towards a bend in the road, and we hear the rattle of wheels, the creak of harness and the drumming of hooves.

It is a public coach, and the roof is laden high with luggage.

Apart from the DRIVER there is another man riding up with him his companion.

As the coach passes camera, the DRIVER whips the horses up to fresh effort.

4. INT. COACH. STUDIO. DAY

The drawn curtains sway with the movement of the coach.

There are five occupants.

Facing backwards are a middle aged MAN and his WIFE, and a fat worried looking MERCHANT.

Facing forwards, one in each corner, with a good space between them is a PRIEST, and JONATHON HARKER.

JONATHON is about thirty years old, pleasant faced and intelligent looking. He is well dressed, and nurses on his lap a small black bag, like a doctor's bag.

There is a certain atmosphere in the coach, rather as though there have been long and heated arguments, and now everyone is resting and restoring themselves for entering the fray once more.

The PRIEST turns towards JONATHON as though to speak, changes his mind and resumes his gazing out of the window.

Then the WIFE leans forward towards JONATHON.

          WIFE:

Young man.......

(3 - 4)

INT. COACH. DAY. (Cont'd)

Her husband reaches out a hand to stop her, but she shakes it free.

                        WIFE:
    .....young man, you have.....you have loved ones
    at home....?

JONATHON looks at her and nods.

                        WIFE:
Then for their sake, if not your own. If the
dictates of reason will not dissuade you, listen
to the dictates of your heart.

                        MAN:
    He's an obstinate you fool.

The WIFE takes not notice of her husband.

                        WIFE:
    Think of how they will suffer....then reconsider.

JONATHON looks at her a moment then smiles.

                        JONATHON:
    I thank you Madam for your concern. But your
    husband is right, I'm an obstinate fool.

                        MERCHANT:
    Mad....mad as hatter.

JONATHON glances towards him with a slight smile, but does not speak.

The PRIEST turns to JONATHON.

                        PRIEST:
    I am a man of God my son. The words that I
    speak are words that I feel in my humble way,
    God might speak.

                        JONATHON:
    If dissuasion is what you wish to speak then
    those will not be the words of God.

                        MERCHANT:
    (to himself) Blasphemous too....mad and blasphemous.

                        MAN:
    You see my dear there is nothing we can do.
    Now please do me a kindness and do not speak
    to this man any more.

INT. COACH. DAY. (Cont'd)

                    PRIEST:
I am not superstitious, my calling should verify that, but I must say to you, that the place to which you go is the gate of hell itself/ The powers of darkness and evil are paramount..... the light of goodness.....

He stops suddenly, as all of them are nearly frightened to death at the appearance of the COMPANION in the trap door. He is leaning down from the front of the coach so all we can see is his head, almost upside down.

He looks towards JONATHON.

                    COMPANION:
(shouts) It's just ahead. You still want to get off?

JONATHON nods and the head of the COMPANION disappears.

5.   <u>EXT. ROAD AND HOUSE OF DRACULA. LOT. DAY.</u>

The house is behind us and we do not see it in this set-up.

The coach rumbles to a halt, with the DRIVER hauling hard on the reins, the brakes screeching.

Before the coach has stopped the COMPANION prepares to jump down.

6.   <u>INT. COACH. DAY.</u>

The other occupants of the coach are sitting in frozen anticipation, as though awaiting the hand of doom. JONATHON is stretching himself preparatory to dismounting from the coach.

He stands and turns to the WIFE and starts to tip his hat.

                    JONATHON:
I thank you madam for your....

But before he can get any further the door behind him is yanked open and the COMPANION reaches inside and drags JONATHON out.

He is helped from the inside by the MERCHANT, who gets to his feet and bids JONATHON farewell with a hearty shove.

7.   <u>EXT. ROAD AND HOUSE OF DRACULA. DAY.</u>

We still do not see the house.

JONATHON barely lands on his feet, still retaining his grip on the black bag. He turns back to the coach as he hits the deck. Even as he does so a large suitcase thuds to the ground at his feet, thrown by the DRIVER.

                                      (5-7)

EXT. ROAD AND HOUSE OF DRACULA. DAY.)Cont'd)

The COMPANION is already climbing back up to the seat next to the DRIVER, and the MERCHANT is leaning out of the window of the coach.

                    MERCHANT:
Alright Coachman....let's get away from here.

The horses are whipped up as he speaks, and he is jerked back out of sight as the couch rumbles off.

As it draws away we see heads stuck from the windows looking back toward JONATHON.

Watching after the coach. There is no resentment in his face. He watches for a moment, then he turns towards the house.

L.S. HOUSE. (possibly MATTE)

The house is a vast rambling affair, a cross between a house and a castle. It is covered with castellated walls and turrets that stick out from the most extraordinary places. The whole place looks as though it has been thrown together rather carelessly with no concessions to planning or convenience.

It has an incredibly bleak aspect, like a place that has been deserted for many years.

L.S. JONATHON.

Standing in the centre of the road, with his large suitcase at his feet, looking towards the House of Dracula.

He looks a small figure, dwarfed by the surroundings.

He picks up his suitcase and starts up the drive.

                    SOFT WIPE TO:

8. <u>EXT. MAUSOLEUM AND DRIVE. LOT. DAY</u>

The mausoleum is at the top of the drive.

JONATHON stops to transfer his heavy suitcase to his other hand. He stares at the gaunt tombs for a moment, then continues his way up to the entrance gates of the House.

9. <u>EXT. COURTYARD AND FRONT DOOR. HOUSE OF DRACULA. LOT. DAY</u>

The whole portice is massive and foreboding. The doors themselves are heavy and scarred with the weather and with age. The door furniture is heavy black metal, and the whole is set back in a deep porch that is reached by a flight of stone steps from the drive.

(8 - 9)

6.

EXT. COURTYARD AND FRONT DOOR. HOUSE OF DRACULA. LOT. DAY (Cont'd)

JONATHON reaches the front door and stops. He puts down his suitcase, stands for a moment, then reaches out for the giant knocker. As he does so there is a flutter of wings and he ducks quickly. There is a momentary shadow of a bat, then it is gone. A second to pull himself together and he wields the knocker. The noise is monumental, but more than that, under the pressure of the knocker one half of the door starts to open.

After a moment, JONATHON pushes it open wider, exposing a stygian darkness inside.

10. INT. HALL OF DRACULA HOUSE. STUDIO. DAY.

The opening door cuts a swathe of weak daylight into the hall, and after a moment the figure of JONATHON steps into the open door, silhouetted against the outside light.

JONATHON looks around him, trying to piece the darkness.

Beyond the swathe of daylight, there is nothing. Just the empty blackness. Then as camera pans taking in what is obviously the entire hall, we see at the far side a glimmer of flickering light, visible through a slit in a barely open door.

JONATHON picks up his suitcase and starts across the hall towards the other door, keeping in that path of light looking through the front door.

He reaches the door, and pushes it open tentatively.

11. INT. DINING ROOM. DRACULA HOUSE. STUDIO. DAY

Looking from the door we see we are in a room which contains a burning fire in a large fireplace across the room in the opposite wall.

In the centre of the room is a table, laid at one end for a meal, with covered dishes, a bottle of wine etc.

The only light is that which comes from the fire, which is burning low.

Then JONATHON, still carrying his suitcase and small bag, comes into the room and walks slowly over to the table.

When he reaches it, he puts down his suitcase and puts the bag on the table, and stands looking around him.

(10 - 11)

INT. DINING ROOM. DRACULA HOUSE. STUDIO. DAY. (Cont'd)

Then he sees on the table, propped against an ornate gold candelabra, an envelope.

He picks this up and looks at the front. Then he reverses it and tears it open.

He takes out a letter and tries to read it, but the light is too bad.

Resting close to the candelabra is a small tinder box. He puts down the letter, strikes a light and lights the two candles in the candelabra.

Then he picks up the letter again, and reads.

12. INSERT

The letter is penned in an ornate and beautifully legible hand.

>   My Dear Harker,
>   I am sorry I was unable to meet you. Eat
>   well, and make yourself comfortable.
>   Count Dracula.

The CAMERA starts to centre on the crest at the head of the paper.

DISSOLVE:

13. INT. DINING ROOM. DRACULA HOUSE. NIGHT.

We Dissolve through to the heavily carved facsimile of the coat of arms. This is on the breastwork of the fireplace.

As we see it there is a shower of sparks from below the frame and a rush of smoke.

We pull back for enough to see JONATHON who has just thrown another log on the fire, which is now blazing merrily.

Having done so he moves back to the table, sits, and pulls his bag towards him. He opens it, and from it he pulls a leather bound diary, and a travelling ink and quill set.

He opens the diary in front of him, then he pushes a couple of dishes aside to make room for the ink stand.

But in doing so, these dishes move against another small stack pushing them from the table

(12 - 13)

INT. DINING ROOM. DRACULA HOUSE. NIGHT. (Cont'd)   8.

The noise in the silence is enormous, and for a moment JONATHON jumps as though he had been shot. Then seeing what has happened he grins slightly at his own nervous state, and gets up from the chair moving around to the side of the table where the dishes have fallen.

There, he goes down on his knees and starts to collect them together again.

C.S. ON FLOOR

JONATHON reaches under the table for the last of the dishes, and pulls it towards him. Then quite suddenly he freezes motionless. Then he looks up.

C.S. WOMAN

From Jonathon's eyeline.

This is an upward angle, dramatising the appearance of the woman.

She is extraordinary beautiful. She is probably about twenty-three or four, and possesses an almost perfect figure.

She is looking down at JONATHON.

TWO SHOT:

After his initial surprise, JONATHON gets to his feet. We see now that what she is wearing leaves very little to the imagination. It is a semi Grecian style gown, cut low in the bodice and gathered at one side of the skirt.

> JONATHON:
> I......I'm sorry.....I didn't hear you come in....
> you startled me I'm afraid.

He realizes he is still carrying a stack of dishes. He puts them down on the table and turns back to the WOMAN, who just continues to look steadily in his direction.

> JONATHON:
> I'm Jonathon Harker.....

He suspends the sentence, waiting for a reaction, but instead of saying anything, the WOMAN turns lightly and moves across to the edge of the table. She runs her hand lightly along the surface, looking down for a moment, then she looks back at JONATHON.

Realising he isn't going to get any help, JONATHON tries again.

> JONATHON:
> Count Dracula left a message for me.......I
> assume he is away on business........

(13)

INT. DINING ROOM. HOUSE OF DRACULA. NIGHT. (Cont'd)

Still nothing from the WOMAN, who continues to look half at JONATHON and half at nothing at all.

By now JONATHON is almost perspiring with embarrassment. Then to his relief the WOMAN steps forward, coming close to him.

              WOMAN:
      Will you tell him you've seen me?

              JONATHON:
      Who?

              WOMAN:
      You mustn't tell him....promise me?

              JONATHON:
      Count Dracula?

The WOMAN nods.

              JONATHON:
      Not if you don't wish me to.

              WOMAN:
      You'll help me won't you?

              JONATHON:
      I'm sorry.....I.....

              WOMAN:
      Say that you'll help me....please.

              JONATHON:
      If there's anything that I can do I'd....

              WOMAN:
      There is....you can help me escape....he never
      lets me go out....I am confined to this house...

JONATHON looks suitably shocked.

              JONATHON:
      That's dreadful....but what can I do?

The WOMAN doesn't answer for a moment, then she takes a step closer to JONATHON.

Suddenly she stops. She hesitates for a moment as if listening then, before JONATHON can do or say anything she moves quickly across the room and out of one of the doors in the fireplace wall.

                                                 (13)

INT. DINING ROOM. HOUSE OF DRACULA. NIGHT. (Cont'd)

JONATHON watches after her a trifle bemused, then he is swung round by a voice.

      DRACULA:
  (off) Harker.....

14 INT. DINING ROOM. HOUSE OF DRACULA. NIGHT

Standing in the door to the hall is COUNT DRACULA

A tall man, his face is thin and saturnine, with deep set eyes, high cheekbones, aquiline nose, high forehead topped by jet black hair.

When he speaks we may notice that his two canine teeth are slightly longer than normal, and definitely more pointed. One gets the impression that unless he makes a conscious effort to the contrary, these teeth would lay along his lower lip. As it is he keeps them well concealed, except when he talks.

He is wearing complete and unrelieved black, a costume cut in the severest lines. Over his suit he wears a long black cloak with a high, pointed collar. He carries a black hat.

For a moment he remains in the doorway motionless, but if he has witnessed the scene with the WOMAN, he makes no sign.

He steps forward into the room with his hand outstretched,

      DRACULA:
  I am glad that you arrived safely my friend.....
  you have eaten well?

JONATHON takes the proffered hand.

      JONATHON:
  Count Dracula?

      DRACULA
  I am Dracula, and I welcome you to my house.
  My deep and sincere apologies that I was not here
  to greet you personally. I trust that you
  found everything that you needed.

      JONATHON
  Thank you sir. It was most thoughtful of you
  to leave a meal for me.

      DRACULA
  I knew that you would be hungry after your
  journey. And tired too I've no doubt.....I
  will show you to your room.

INT. DINING ROOM. HOUSE OF DRACULA. NIGHT. (Cont'd)

He starts towards the staircase.

                DRACULA:
(Cont'd) ......it is most unfortunate that I have to go again immediately. Your impressions of me as a host must be abysmal, but what I must do is unavoidable.

JONATHON has started to gather his bags and cloak. But when he goes to pick up his large suitcase, DRACULA beats him to it.

                DRACULA:
Please, allow me....

We have perhaps noticed that this suitcase is obviously heavy by the manner in which JONATHON has carried it heretonow, always putting it down when he gets the opportunity. But Dracula takes it up as though it weighed nothing, swinging it in front of him as he moves up the stairs.

                DRACULA:
There are a great number of volumes to be indexed. Tomorrow, I shall show you the library where you are to work.

                JONATHON:
I will do the best I can sir.

                DRACULA:
I am sure that you will, and I count myself lucky that I have obtained the services of so noteworthy a scholar to act as my librarian.

                JONATHON:
As I told you sir in my letter, it will be a pleasure for me to be able to stay here where it is quiet and peaceful. The work that I shall do on your behalf is small payment for the seclusion that your house offers.

                DRACULA:
Then we are both satisfied....and admirable arrangement.....

15.   INT. PASSAGE AND STAIRS. NIGHT.

We are in a short passage, from which leads another run of stairs and at least one door.

When JONATHON comes into the passage, DRACULA is already standing at a door at the head of the stairs. He is holding the door open, waiting for JONATHON to precede him through.

(14 - 15)

INT. PASSAGE & STAIRS. (CONT'D)

JONATHON passes through the door in front of DRACULA.
DRACULA goes in after him.

Then we see at the end of the passage, a door which up to now has seemed closed like the others, move tightly shut, showing that it was in fact sufficiently open for someone to have peered out.

16. INT. JONATHON'S BEDROOM. STUDIO. NIGHT.

This is another large room. Here too, a fire is burning in the grate.

Against one wall is a large four poster, which is turned down ready for occupation.

There is a table in the centre of the room, and two wing chairs either side of the fireplace.

There is a window in one wall, though at the moment curtains are drawn across it.

DRACULA has placed JONATHON'S suitcase on a small table by the side of the bed, and he is watching JONATHON who is putting his little black bag on the table in the centre of the room.

As JONATHON has only just replaced the diary and ink stand, the bag has not been shut, and it is on the table, gaping open.

DRACULA moves across to where JONATHON is standing.

> DRACULA:
> I hope that you will be comfortable here, and now I must leave you. One more thing before I go, the errand that calls me out now is such that I will not be returning until after sundown tomorrow.

As he talks he glances down at JONATHON'S bag on the table.

He looks up at JONATHON.

> DRACULA:
> ....your permission?

DRACULA reaches into the bag, and from the bag DRACULA pulls a framed picture, and the DIARY. He holds the diary for a moment, then he puts it down and looks at the picture.

> DRACULA
> This is charming....quite charming.....

(15 - 16)

13.

17. INSERT

In the frame is a picture of a very lovely lady, who we later learn is LUCY.

18. INT. JONATHON'S BEDROOM. NIGHT.

> DRACULA:
> You are fortunate indeed to own acquaintance with such a lovely young person.......

He looks at JONATHON.

> ......your wife perhaps?

> JONATHON:
> My fiancee, Miss Lucy Holmwood.

> DRACULA:
> Lucy....what a delightful name...

He puts the picture down on the table, pushing the Diary aside to do so,

> .....well I must leave you now my friend. Once again accept my sincere apologies for the sad way I have been forced to neglect my duties as host...

He moves over to the door, then turns to face JONATHON.

> ...good night to you........ and I trust that you will sleep well.

Then he is gone.

JONATHON stands for a moment looking after him.

Then there is the unmistakable sound of a key turning in the door outside.

He moves across to the door quickly and tries it. Sure enough it is locked.

He turns away from the door and looks round the room. There is no other door.

After a moment he moves across to the curtains and lifting one of them aside, he peers out.

19. EXT. WINDOW OF BEDROOM. STUDIO. NIGHT.

JONATHON looks down at the drive.

(17 - 19)

14.

20.   EXT. MAUSOLEUM AND DRIVE. LOT. NIGHT.

It is a filthy night - the wind picking up the dry leaves and blowing them about.

21.   EXT. WINDOW OF BEDROOM. NIGHT.

JONATHON is about to turn from the window back into the room, when he stops, and looks out again.

22.   EXT. MAUSOLEUM AND DRIVE. NIGHT.

What has caught his eye is the fact that the door, which is three quarters facing him, has started to open, pushed from the inside.

After a moment there appears in the door, the cloaked figure of DRACULA.

He pushes the door shut behind him then cuts across the grounds to the drive.

There, he starts up the drive, the wind catching in his cloak and billowing it up behind him until it is level and occasionally above his shoulders.

He walks quickly, and this combined with the winged effect of his billowing cloak creates the impression of a giant bat flying along almost at ground level.

He moves on along the drive towards the Main Gates, where we see him go out.

23.   INT. JONATHON'S BEDROOM. NIGHT

JONATHON remains at the curtains looking for a moment longer, then he lets the curtain drop back into place.

After a moment he starts over to the table where he draws up a chair and sits down.

Then he takes his diary and ink well from his bag and sets them out in front of him.

He opens the diary to a fresh page, dips his pen in the ink, and after a seconds thought, he starts writing.

As he does so we Fade in his voice over.

      JONATHON'S VOICE:
  At last I have met Count Dracula. He accepts
  me as a man who has agreed to work among his

(20 - 23)

INT. JONATHON'S BEDROOM. NIGHT. (Cont'd)

> JONATHON'S VOICE:
> (Cont'd) books, as I intended. It only remains for me now to await the daylight hours, when with God's help I will forever end this man's reign of terror.

DISSOLVE:

24. INT. JONATHON'S BEDROOM. NIGHT.

C.S. JONATHON

He is dozing having fallen asleep by the fire.

C.S. DOOR

The door handle starts to turn slowly as though someone is attempting to open it from the outside.

Then the handle stops turning, returns to normal, and there is the unmistakable click of the lock of being turned.

C.S. JONATHON

He wakes suddenly, and after a beat, he gets to his feet and moves across to the door quickly. Then quietly and carefully he turns the handle and suddenly pulls the door open.

There is no-one there, and he advances into the passage.

25. INT. PASSAGE AND STAIRS. NIGHT.

JONATHON comes out and looks down the stairs. At one end even as he looks, he sees a door close softly. This was the door we saw move when JONATHON and DRACULA entered the bedroom.

JONATHON starts down the stairs towards the door he saw closing.

Reaching it, he hesitated for a second, then tries the handle.

The door opens easily, and throwing it back, looks into the room beyond.

26. INT. GOTHIC ROOM. STUDIO. NIGHT.

This is a vast room, completely bare and empty.

To one side there is a large stained glass window, designed like that in a church, although there is no discernible motive in the pattern of the glass. The moonlight through this is the only light sources.

After a moment JONATHON steps fully into the room.

(23 - 26)

16.

INT. GOTHIC ROOM. STUDIO. NIGHT. (Cont'd)

He takes a couple of steps forward, then a small sound from behind him makes him swing round.

Standing against the wall, behind the door is the WOMAN he saw earlier. Now, in the subdued light of the moon, she looks even more attractive than she did before.

She is still bare footed and wearing the same revealing gown.

JONATHON is about to say something to her when she holds up a finger to her lips.

JONATHON stops, and watches while she comes from behind the door, looks into the passage, then quickly closes the door and turns to face him again.

          WOMAN:
    You will help me won't you?

         JONATHON:
    Why is the Count keeping you prisoner?

          WOMAN:
    I can't tell you that.

JONATHON hesitates for a moment.

         JONATHON:
    Then I can't help you.

          WOMAN:
    You're not.......not one of....

She pauses.

         JONATHON
    One of what?

The WOMAN shakes her head.

          WOMAN:
    No, you couldn't be.....

She reaches out a hand and touches his arm.

          WOMAN:
    ....you're strong...

         JONATHON:
    I must know why he is keeping you prisoner.

                (26)

INT. GOTHIC ROOM. NIGHT. (Cont'd)

Suddenly she blazes.

> WOMAN:
> Why? What difference can it make? Is it not sufficient that he keeps me locked up....? that he starved me....? Then he.....(she calms down). You cannot imagine what he is like -...the terrible things he does. I live with fear all the time...I dare not try to escape on my own...he would find me wherever I hid.....bring me back here. He is a foul wicked man.....you will help me....say that you will, there is nothing I can do against him..... you are strong....you can fight him....

Her voice is rising toward Hysteria.

> WOMAN:
> ....you must...you don't know what he will do to me if I can't get away...you've got to help me... you must....you must....you must....

As she reaches the last, she grabs the lapels of his coat and starts to shake him for emphasis, pleading.

JONATHON grabs for her hands with his and pulls them from his coat.

He stands looking at her for a moment, and she at him. A long moment.

> JONATHON:
> I'll help you....I promise.

Tears of relief swell into her eyes, and she closes the small intervening gap between them and nestles her head on his chest.

One hand circles her shoulders and he starts to pat her rather clumsily on the back.

> WOMAN:
> Oh thank you...thank you....you'll never regret this....never....what you have done you'll remember to your dying day.

C.S. JONATHON

Looking across the top of her head, a look of compassion on his face.

C.S. WOMAN

Her head is sideways on his chest with her cheek resting against

(26)

INT. GOTHIC ROOM. NIGHT. (Cont'd)

him. We can see JONATHON'S neck running out of frame,

The tears have stopped now and she is cradling her head gratefully secure in the thought of masculine assistance.

Then her eyes slide sideways until she is looking towards JONATHON, and towards his neck.

It starts with a twitch of the upper lip, an incontrollable impulse. Then the upper lip starts to curl back like that of a snarling animal, and we see the two long, sharp canine teeth.

Much too long and too sharp to belong to a normal person.

Then she shifts head sideways a fraction as though to bury her face deeper into his chest, reaches up slightly and places the two canine teeth softly onto the bare flesh of his neck.

The two teeth make tiny indentations in the flesh, then waiting for a fraction, she suddenly winks her teeth deep into him.

At the same time there is a scream of anger from off.

JONATHON pushes the WOMAN away from him violently, and both he and the WOMAN turn towards the noise.

Standing in the door is DRACULA.

He is livid with rage. But also he is livid with something else. His whole face is puffy, especially around the jaws, and un-naturally ruddy. From either side of his mouth there runs a trickle of blood. His clothes, although black. manage to show in great damp smears, where blood has spilled and streaked across his person.

Even as we see this, he steps forward where the WOMAN is cowering a little way from JONATHON.

Ignoring JONATHON he reaches out and grabs the WOMAN by the hair with one hand. Then he yanks hard sending the WOMAN spinning across the room with a scream of pain where she lands on the floor.

Immediately she gets to her feet again, and starts towards the two men. But it is not DRACULA she heads for, it is JONATHON. She ignores DRACULA as she passes him towards JONATHON.

JONATHON puts up his hands to fend off the barrage, but before she can quite reach him DRACULA intervenes again.

Furious, he grasps her by the shoulder and spins her round but she wriggles herself free from his grip and again turns towards JONATHON. She is a wild thing now, her lips drawn back, her hair bedraggled and falling across the front of her face.

(26)

19.

INT. GOTHIC ROOM. NIGHT. (Cont'd)

DRACULA reaches out again and grabs her by the hair. Then as before he yanks hard and sends her spinning across the room. She lands on the floor, but this time makes no attempt to get to her feet. She rests on her arms looking towards DRACULA through a tangle of hair.

Now DRACULA starts towards her. It is obvious by the menace in his movement that he intends to do something pretty brutal to the WOMAN, and JONATHON pulls himself together and makes the first move he has done since DRACULA came into the room.

He moves up behind DRACULA and grabs his arm.

                    JONATHON:
  Don't do........

But DRACULA shakes his hand away, almost unaware that it was placed there, and continues towards the WOMAN.

But JONATHON moves up behind DRACULA again, and as DRACULA starts to bend over the WOMAN, JONATHON reaches with his arms around DRACULA and drags him backwards.

For a moment it seems as though DRACULA still isn't going to take any notice. Then he straightens up, and sweeping his arms wide he breaks JONATHON'S hold as though JONATHON was a child.

JONATHON is sent rocking back a couple of paces. Then DRACULA turns to face him.

Before JONATHON can move or say anything DRACULA reaches but one hand and grabs JONATHON by the throat.

C.S. JONATHON

The spidery hand of DRACULA is around his throat, the long fingers sinking into the flesh.

JONATHON'S eyes start to bulge as he puts his two hands up and tries to break DRACULA'S grip.

But it is useless, the grip is like iron.

C.S. DRACULA

He is looking along his arm at JONATHON.

His expression is quite murderous, his lip is drawn back exposing his two long canine teeth, and the blood still staining his chin.

(26)

20.

INT. GOTHIC ROOM. NIGHT. (Cont'd)

C.S. JONATHON

We see his hands fall away as DRACULA increases the pressure on his throat and gradually JONATHON starts to lose consciousness.

C.S. DRACULA

Gradually the face of DRACULA starts to swim out of focus, then it comes back in again, then starts out once more.

M.S.

DRACULA suddenly shoots out his arm, the one holding JONATHON to it's full extent, and lets go of JONATHON's throat at the same time.

JONATHON goes hurtling across the room and fetches up hard against the far wall, where he sinks to the floor.

C.S. JONATHON

He rolls over on the floor and then tries to struggle to his elbows. A sharp scream from the WOMAN out of shot focuses his bleary gaze in that direction.

M.S. DRACULA AND WOMAN.

Whatever it is that DRACULA did that caused the WOMAN to scream, has also caused her to lose conciousness.

He has picked her up and is carrying her towards the door.

Just before going through DRACULA stops for a beat and looks across at JONATHON. Then he goes through.

C.S. JONATHON

He starts to try and struggle to his feet.

He manages to get on all fours, then he collapses as we:

                        TRICK DISSOLVE TO:

27. INT. JONATHON'S BEDROOM. DAY.

C.S. JONATHON

He is laying on the floor, looking rather battered after his ordeal.

Then his eyes open and he takes a moment to orientate himself.

                        (26-27)

INT. JONATHON'S BEDROOM. DAY. (Cont'd)

The curtains are still drawn, and the fire in the grate has gone out. His diary still lays open on the page where he was working last night. Everything is as he left it.

Then in a rush he remembers what has happened to him.

He gets to his feet quickly and moves over to the door. He tries the handle, but it is locked. He tugs the door for a second trying to get it open, then he moves back to the table where he has left his small black bag.

He rummages in this for a second and comes up with a small shaving mirror.

He hold this up and looks into it.

Then his hand goes to his next and he fingers the two puckered sores under his chin, where even now the blood is still leading from, down to the collar of his jacket.

He puts the mirror down and hurries over to the window where he pulls aside the curtains. The late afternoon sunlight streams in.

He looks at his watch quickly, as he walks back to the table. There he sits and pulls his Diary toward him. He starts writing.

As he does so we fade in JONATHON'S voice:

                    JONATHON'S VOICE:
    The worst has happened....I have myself become the
    victim of the vampire. Should misfortune continue
    to befall me and I am unable to carry out my task
    I can only pray that whoever finds my body will
    possess the knowledge to do what is necessary to
    release my soul, and prevent me from becoming one
    of them.........

                    DISSOLVE:

Shooting onto window where the sun is even lower. After a moment JONATHON comes into frame and we carry over his voice from the preceding page.

He looks out.

                    JONATHON'S VOICE:
    While my senses are still my own I must do
    what I set out to do.....

We see that he is carrying the Diary and a small canvas pack.

INT. JONATHON'S BEDROOM. DAY. (Cont'd)

He starts to cock his leg over the windowsill.

>   JONATHON'S VOICE:
> (Cont'd) I must find the resting place of Dracula
> and there end his existence forever.......

DISSOLVE:

28. EXT. DRIVE. HOUSE OF DRACULA. DAY. (SUNSET EFFECT)

JONATHON is hurrying down the drive towards the main gates.

His voice still continues over as we see him glance upwards to the rapidly disappearing sun.

>   JONATHON'S VOICE:
> ......soon it will be sundown and they will walk
> again...I do not have much time.

29. EXT. ROAD AND HOUSE OF DRACULA. DAY. (SUNSET EFFECT)

He moves out through the gate until he is standing in the road.

He looks up and down, there is no-one in sight. Then he moves across the road and a slight way down from the gates and going close to a tree, he places his diary in the crotch of a branch that overhangs the road.

He steps back to see if this is visible to anyone passing along the road, then satisfied he moves back towards the gates.

SOFT WIPE TO:

30. EXT. DRACULA MAUSOLEUM. DAY. (SUNSET EFFECT)

JONATHON looks up at the sun once more, then starts towards the Mausoleum.

C.S. MAUSOLEUM. DOOR.

JONATHON comes into pictures, and moves to the door to the mausoleum. It looks as though it is permanently shut and weathered into place.

But JONATHON knows better. He puts his shoulder against the door and it gives slightly.

Standing back he starts to run his hand up the edge of the cornice, looking for a catch.

After a few moments he finds what he is looking for and the door swings silently outwards,

(27 - 30)

23.

EXT. DRACULA MAUSOLEUM. DAY. (SUNSET EFFECT) (Cont'd)

Hefting his roll in his hand, JONATHON steps into the gloom.

31. INT. DRACULA MAUSOLEUM. DAY. (SUNSET)

The only light is a shaft of hard sun through the open door, and this seems to be swallowed up in the stygian gloom that pervades the entire mausoleum.

The two coffins that we saw earlier still rest quietly where they were, and it seems that the dust of ages lies around and over everything.

Slowly JONATHON approaches the coffins, he goes to the larger one first, and after steeling himself, he suddenly throws back the lid.

C.S. DRACULA

He is laying there, eyes shut. All the sins of the world are etched in the lines of his face. In his relaxed position the two long canines are plainly visible, and there are still smears of blood on his face.

C.S. JONATHON

He looks for a moment longer, then turns to the smaller of the two coffins. He throws back the lid of this one too.

C.S. WOMAN

She too is lying with her eyes closed. Her expression is that of a well fed cat. A trickle of blood runs from the corner of her mouth, down her neck and across the upper portion of her breasts.

Even with the complete relaxation, the deathlike trance, she still looks eminently desirable.

C.S. JONATHON

He takes his roll, and untying the cords that hold it he rolls it out on the edge of the plinth of the smaller coffin.

It exposes a short handled, iron headed hammer, and a number of needle sharp wooden stakes, about a foot long.

He takes the hammer in his right hand, and one of the stakes in his left, then he steps closer to the WOMAN'S coffin.

Then he leans over the coffin.

(30 - 31)

24.

INT. DRACULA MAUSOLEUM. DAY. (SUNSET) (Cont'd)

C.S. WOMAN

JONATHON'S hand comes into frame, the one holding the sharpened stake.

He places the point just under the WOMAN'S left breast, and we see it hollow an indentation in the skin.

C.S. JONATHON ACROSS COFFIN.

We are shooting across the top of the open coffin lid, and can see JONATHON'S upper body as he stands on the far side of the raised lid.

We see him steel himself, then raise his right hand, the one with the hammer.

After a moments pause, he brings it down hard onto the stake, out of picture.

There is a sudden shattering scream of agony, but JONATHON doesn't falter. He brings the hammer down again, and then again.

Then he steps back weakly watching what is happening in the coffin.

The noise is indescribable, a half scream, a half moan, which after a while starts to diminish to a whimper.

C.S. DRACULA.

He is still as we saw him last, but quite suddenly his eyes begin to open, and he rolls his head sideways.

C.S. JONATHON'S BACK.

DRACULA'S eyeline. Then the eyeline switches slightly and moves over to a small window. The red of the sunset has gone, and already it is twilight.

C.S. JONATHON.

He is still looking down into the coffin of the WOMAN. The noise has almost completely died out now, and then with a small whimper there is silence.

JONATHON leans forward and looks into the coffin more closely.

Where there was a beautiful young girl, there is now the body of a very, very old woman. Still dressed in what the girl was wearing, she lays there almost crumpling before our eyes, so old is she.

(31)

25.

INT. DRACULA MAUSOLEUM. DAY. (SUNSET) (Cont'd)

C.S. WOMAN

We can see the end of the stake protruding from her breast.

Then cutting across the shot, the lid of the coffin closes.

C.S. JONATHON

Having closed the lid, he still stands there a moment getting over the horror of his experience.

Then realising he has not finished, he takes another stake and turns to the coffin of DRACULA.

Then he freezes to immobility.

C.S. COFFIN

It is empty. An indentation in the soil that lays at the bottom of the coffin showing where the Count lay.

C.S. JONATHON

He stares, unable to believe his eyes, then a sound pulls him round sharply.

EYELINE TO DOOR.

The door of the mausoleum is just swinging shut. Even as we see it, it slams hard with a solid clunk, and practically all light is cut off.

After a moment there is a shuffle of feet, a small gasp. Then there is silence again.

The silence stretches and stretches for as long as it cam be held.

Then there is a scream, a wild pain filled scream, that pierces the silence like a knife.

On the high point of this scream we

                        DISSOLVE:

32. INT. INN. DAY.

This is the tap room of the local Inn, situated at the nearest town or village to the House of Dracula.

There is a crude bar down one side, and either side of the fireplace there are high back wing benches

(31 - 32)

26.

INT. INN. DAY (Cont'd)

There are perhaps half a dozen men standing at one end of the bar, while at the other end is VAN HELSING. The LANDLORD stands behind the bar, and his position makes it obvious that he is with the half a dozen as opposed to HELSING.

HELSING is a tall, well built man, with a lean distinguished face. He is immaculately dressed although not sporting any particular fripperies in his costume, rather is it a sober colour and slightly severely cut outfit.

HELSING is talking to the others. Whatever it is he's trying to find out he isn't having much success and his patience is beginning to wear thin, and he is getting very angry.

>	HESLING:
>	I am simply asking you to tell me where he went when he left here....can't you get it into you heads that's all i want to know.

He looks at the men, staring at each one for a moment, then passing onto the next. They all regard him in a mute truculence, and not a little fear. He relaxes slightly...perhaps a little ashamed at having insulted them.

>	HESLING:
>	I will start again at the beginning.....

He taps a letter that is laying on the counter in front of him.

>	.....I have a letter dated three days ago, from a Jonathon Harker. He says he is going to stop here overnight and is due to catch the postchaise tomorrow... Did he or did he not cat the postchaise? And if he did, which direction did he take......?

Still there is nothing from the men.

>	HESLING:
>	(shouts) I must know where he went.

The LANDLORD takes a step forward.

>	LANDLORD:
>	Look, whoever you are. You came in this place after information. We can't give it you. Now why don't you leave us alone.

>	HESLING:
>	I cannot leave you alone.....this is a matter of life or death. For the last time.....where did Jonathon Harker go when he left here?

(32)

INT. INN. DAY. (Cont'd)

                    LANDLORD:
          (angry now) And for the last time...we don't know
          nothing about it.

Suddenly HELSING straightens up and strides across to the window
set just to the left of the door. The window frame is hung with
strings of garlic.

He reaches up and tears down one of these strings.

                    LANDLORD:
          Hey....what are....?

HELSING turns towards him with the string of garlic in his hand.

                    HESLING:
          Look at this....garlic.....here to...

He points to the top of the door where there is more garlic strung
along.

          ....everywhere garlic.

He throws the string of garlic onto the floor and comes back to
the bar. All the men are watching him very closely now.

                    HELSING:
          Why is that garlic kept there?

                    LANDLORD:
          It's drying...

                    HESLING:
          It's there as a protection. It's your protection
          against Vampires....we all know vampires cannot
          tolerate garlic. But can't you get it into you
          thick heads that the information I'm seeking could
          end forever this....this terror you live in.
          Jonathon Harker came here to help you....I must
          know where he was going if I am to finish the work
          he started.

                    LANDLORD:
          It should never have been started...there are some
          things that are best left undone....now leave us
          alone...we will tell you nothing.

He turns away from HELSING as do the others, and finally HELSING
relaxes inside of himself and starts across towards the fire.

(32)

INT. INN DAY. (Cont'd)

                HESLING:
Bring me some supper.

                LANDLORD:
(shouting) Inga.....

He shouts in the direction of the kitchen door which stands open.

After a moment a pretty young girl sticks her head out of the kitchen

                LANDLORD:
Bring him some supper.

The head disappears.

Meanwhile HESLING has moved over to one of the high backed benches by the fire.

HESLING slips off his cloak, and hangs it over the back of the bench, then he sits.

He pulls the letter out again and reads it, his brow furrowed with worry and concentration, then he looks up as INGA comes round from the back of the bench carrying a tray with the cutlery etcetera for his supper.

We notice that where HESLING is sitting is completely screened from the rest of the bar.

He smiles a little tiredly at INGA as he starts to put the letter back in his pocket, then he notices INGA is looking at him hard, trying to pass some sort of a signal.

She has put the tray down on the table beside him, now she leans close to him.

                INGA:
This was found and brought here...nobody
can read it....they told me to burn it....
but he...he was such a kind gentleman...

She lifts the corner of the napkin on the tray. There is the Diary.

Then as he smiles his thanks to INGA, she moves away.

Checking that he cannot be seen, he slips the Diary out from under the napkin, and flips open the cover,

                          (32)

INT. INN. DAY (Cont'd)

Written on the fly leaf is:

    The Diary of Jonathon Harker.

                              DISSOLVE:

33. EXT. ROAD AND HOUSE OF DRACULA. DAY.

We are outside the main Gates, which now stand fully open.

After a moment the figure of VAN HESLING moves into shot.

He is about to go through the gates when there is the sound of a shout and the crack of a whip from inside the gates, followed by the rumbling of wheels.

Suddenly HESLING jumps back into the protection of the gate pillars as from the drive there rumbles a huge horse drawn hearse.

It is being driven fast by an obviously terrified man, who doesn't even see HESLING. The hearse is drawn by two huge drey horses, coal black with high nodding plumes on their foreheads.

Through the undrawn curtains into the hearse proper we can see a large ornate coffin which is slipping and sliding from side to side with the momentum of the hearse.

The hearse turns out of the gates, rocks round onto the road and thunders off down the tree lined avenue sending up clouds of dust.

HESLING steps back into the road and looks off after the hearse for a moment, then he turns and starts through the gates.

34. EXT. DRIVE. DAY.

In the drive he starts up towards the house,

(33 - 34)

34. EXT. DRIVE. DAY (CONT'D)

After a few paces something off shot catches his eye.

35. EXT. DRACULA MAUSOLEUM. DAY.

From his eyeline we can see the mausoleum, the door of which stands open.

36. EXT. DRIVE. DAY.

After a moment HESLING turns and continues his way up the drive.

37. EXT. COURTYARD AND FRONT DOOR OF HOUSE OF DRACULA. DAY.

HESLING comes into shot.

The door stands half-open, and HESLING gives it a push and steps onto the threshold.

38. INT. DINING ROOM. HOUSE OF DRACULA. DAY.

Shooting towards the door that leads to the Hall.

After a moment there appears in the door the figure of HESLING. He looks around him.

The dining room is as we last saw it, the dirty dishes that JONATHON left after his dinner, remaining untouched.

HESLING enters the room and calls.

     HESLING
 (Calling) Harker.

He is answered by a faint echo. He calls again, louder.

     HESLING
 (calls) Harker

Still just the echo. He crosses to the stairs and starts to walk up them.

39. INT. PASSAGE. DAY

He comes into the passage, looks around him. The door of JONATHON's bedroom stand open.

He goes across and into JONATHON's bedroom.

40. INT. JONATHON'S BEDROOM. DAY.

This room too is exactly as it was when we last saw it, except for JONATHON's belongings. The cases are open and their contents are strewn around them. The lining of the cases too has been ripped out.

(34 - 40)

40. INT. JONATHON'S BEDROOM. DAY. (Cont'd)

    HESLING moves into the room, then something catches his eye.

    Standing on the table is the frame that held the picture of LUCY. He picks it up and looks at it.

41. INSERT

    The frame is still intact ... but it is empty. The photograph has been torn out of it.

                                        QUICK DISSOLVE.

42. EXT. DRACULA MAUSOLEUM. DAY.

    HESLING comes into frame and stops outside the door. After a moment he steps into the Mausoleum.

43. INT. DRACULA MAUSOLEUM. DAY

    Inside things are as they always were, the two coffins resting on their respective plinths.

    HESLING moves over to the smaller of the two, and tries the lid tentatively. It opens and he looks in.

    C.S. WOMAN

    There is the old, old woman, complete with stake through her heart.

    C.S. HESLING

    He looks at her for a moment, then he lowers the lid and turns to the other coffin.

    He opens this one too, then gasps with horror at what he sees.

    C.S. JONATHON

    Resting where DRACULA has rested is what remains of JONATHON HARKER.

    Completely drained of all blood, what is left is merely skin over a skeleton. The skeleton hands are crossed in mock reverence over the chest, and the skull grins up at HESLING malevolently.

    C.S. HESLING

    He is looking down at the body of JONATHON, then he bends closer.

                                        (40 - 43)

INT. DRACULA MAUSOLEUM. DAY. (Cont'd)

C.S. JONATHON

A closer shot of what is left of JONATHON shows the marks on the skin of his neck. The marks of the vampire.

C.S. HELSING

He straightens up slowly, and we Fade in the voice of JONATHON

> JONATHON'S VOICE:
> ....I can only pray that whoever discovers
> my body will have the knowledge to do what
> is necessary to release my soul, thereby
> preventing me from becoming one of them...

Almost as though he has heard JONATHON talking, HESLING looks down at the coffin again.

Then he turns and look round the mausoleum.

Immediately he sees the Hammer and Stake that JONATHON was going to use. He bends down to pick them up and we:

> DISSOLVE:

44. INT. SITTING ROOM. STUDIO. DAY.

This is the sitting room of the Holmwood's house. It is comfortably furnished in the best of taste, contrasting with the bleak severity of the House of Dracula.

The style of furniture and dressing tells us that we are still on the Continent.

We see VAN HESLING, overcoated, his hat on a nearby chain. He stands talking to ARTHUR and MINA HOLMWOOD.

> HESLING:
> I realise how fantastic my request must sound,
> but I must ask you once again not to press me
> for details of Jonathon's death.

> ARTHUR:
> You mean you still refuse to tell us..

> HESLING:
> I'm afraid that is so.

> ARTHUR:
> I won't accept your refusal.

(43 - 44)

INT. SITTING ROOM. STUDIO. DAY. (Cont'd)

MINA rests her hand on her husband's arm.

MINA:
(gently) Arthur.

ARTHUR:
No, Mina....please allow me to handle this (to Hesling) I find your whole story of Jonathon's death suspicious in the extreme. You come here and tell us that he is dead, then you refuse to tell us the manner in which he died. How are we to know you are telling the truth? Perhaps he is not dead at all.

HESLING:
(coldly) You have the death certificate.

ARTHUR waves the paper he holds in his hand.

ARTHUR:
'Death by natural causes'....and signed by you. I'm afraid that is just not good enough.

MINA:
Doctor Hesling how long ago was it?

HESLING:
Ten days ago. I would have let you know......

ARTHUR:
Ten days! Then why have we not received his body?

HESLING:
(a beat) The body of Jonathon Harker was cremated, Mr. Holmwood.

ARTHUR:
Cremated! By whose authority?

HESLING:
Mine.

This is too much for ARTHUR:

ARTHUR:
You're out of your mind....you're insane.

MINA:
Arthur!

MINA stands up between the two men.

INT. SITTING ROOM. STUDIO. DAY. (Cont'd)

>MINA:
>You must forgive my husband, Doctor Hesling.
>You must also appreciate his feelings.

>HESLING:
>(to Mina) Be assured that I do. In return,
>I must ask you to appreciate mine. Jonathon
>Harker and I were very close friends. His death
>was possibly more of a loss to me than... to
>either of you.

MINA senses his sincerity.

>MINA:
>I'm sorry.

>HESLING:
>(to Arthur) Now may I remind you that it was not
>you, nor your charming wife I came to see, but
>Jonathon's fiancee, your sister Lucy?

>ARTHUR:
>I forbid you to see my sister.

>HESLING:
>(a beat) That is up to you of course. If you
>refuse me permission to see her then I must accept
>that refusal.

He turns to MINA

>HESLING:
>I trust that Miss Lucy will not suffer to much
>at the news of her fiancee's death (to Arthur)
>I can show myself out.

He leaves.

>ARTHUR:
>I shall report his actions to the police.

>MINA:
>Arthur, dear, he is Doctor Van Hesling, a lecturer
>at Utrecht University and one of the most respected
>men in his own country.

ARTHUR is about to intercept, but MINA stops him.

>MINA:
>He was also one of Jonathon's closest friends.

ARTHUR is deflated.   (44)

INT. SITTING ROOM. STUDIO. DAY. (Cont'd)

        MINA:
And he had ridden more than a hundred miles to see us Arthur - and to break the news to Lucy.

        ARTHUR:
Mina, Lucy is sick.

        MINA:
She will have to learn sometime, Arthur.

        ARTHUR:
But from us Mina - not from him. We'll see how she is the evening - decide then.

        DISSOLVE:

THERE IS NO SCENE NO. 45.

46. <u>INT. LUCY'S BEDROOM. NIGHT</u>

This is a ground floor room with wide French Windows leading onto a patio and to the garden beyond.

There is a feminine touch to the room in the chines and drapes, and the matching dressing table.

In a bed, set against one wall, sits LUCY.

She is a very beautiful young lady, although now she looks as though she is just recovering from a long illness.

She is propped up with pillows behind her back and she is looking at MINA and ARTHUR who are standing at the foot of her bed.

        LUCY:
It is a premonition I have...I know that he will be home soon....

She smiles a delightful smile.

        ....go on you two, put it down to the delirious
        ravings....Jonathon will be home inside of
        a week. Then we'll see how long I remain an
        invalid.....I won't need old pompous doctor
        Seward to tell me he doesn't know what's wrong
        with me....

(44 & 46)

INT. LUCY'S BEDROOM. NIGHT. (Cont'd)

ARTHUR and MINA don't say a word. Finally MINA smiles and steps forward.

          MINA:
Of course dear. Why don't you lie down now and try to go to sleep....here, let me take one of those pillows.

MINA removes a pillow from behind LUCY'S back and LUCY sinks back.

MINA bends forward and kisses LUCY on the forehead.

          MINA:
Good night dear.

          LUCY:
Good night Mina....good night Arthur...and stop standing there like a big brother.....looking all ferocious.

Suddenly on an impulse ARTHUR comes round the side of the bed and he too kisses LUCY on the forehead.

          LUCY:
My, we are affectionate this evening. Now why don't the two of you go into the parlour and turn down the lights....or has the novelty worn off after a month of wedded bliss. It won't with Jonathon and me....you see.

Another look flashes between MINA and ARTHUR. The time LUCY intercepts it.

          LUCY:
What's the matter with you two this evening .....you're like a couple of old bears.

          MINA:
It's nothing dear, you're imagining things. Now try and get some sleep.

The two of them move over to the door from the bedroom, MINA picking up the lamp en route.

They stop at the door and turn to LUCY again.

          MINA:
Good night dear.

                                  (46)

INT. LUCY'S BEDROOM. NIGHT. (Cont'd)

                    ARTHUR:
    Good night Lucy

                    LUCY:
    Good night both of you.

They exit.

As the door closes quietly behind them LUCY'S pose of apparent lightheartedness seems to drop off her and she rolls over on the pillow looking towards the French Windows, through which the moonlight streams.

C.S. LUCY

On her neck, plainly visible are two puncture marks. The mark of the Vampire.

She lay there a moment looking out of the window, then after a slight pause, she sits up.

She throws back the bedclothes and slips out of bed. There is a dressing gown at the foot of her bed, but she doesn't bother with this.

In her extremely diaphanous and low cut nightgown, she goes straight to the door of the room.

There she presses her ear up against the door for a second, and hearing nothing she straightens up.

Then she puts out her hand and turns the key in the lock, silently so that the click is barely audible.

Then she starts over towards the French Windows. Her movements are almost hypnotic.

She stands by the French Windows for a moment, then she leans forward and unlocks them. Then she pulls them open.

A breath of night air caresses the hem of her night gown and she shivers uncontrollably, then she steps back a pace looking toward the open French Window.

Then she turns and starts back toward the bed.

She reaches the edge of the bed, and raising her arms she undoes the small clip on the gold chain that bears a crucifix which hangs round her neck.

(46)

INT. LUCY'S BEDROOM. NIGHT. (Cont'd)

She takes the crucifix and lays it on the bedside table.

Then she eases the nightdress from her shoulders and lays down on the bed, looking towards the open French Windows as we:

        DISSOLVE:

47. INT. HESLING'S HOTEL SUITE. NIGHT.

This is a suite at what is obviously the best hotel in Town.

The camera features what must be one of the original Dictaphone recording machines. The framework is of wrought-iron and the black recording cylinder wobbles slightly on its axis, causing the needle to rock up and down as it follows the groove.

The scratchy voice which comes from the hown barely recognizable as that of VAN HESLING, whom the camera discovers leaning against the wall, smoking an ornate pipe and listening intently to his record of all that the saw at Castle Dracula.

     HESLING:
  (distorted voice) ....on entering the bedroom,
  I discovered Jonathon Harker's belongings strewn
  across the room. The lining of his bag had been
  torn out in a manner to suggest that someone had
  been making a desperate search for something.
  For what......? For Jonathon's diary?.......

HESLING has crossed to the table on which are set out all HARKER'S belongings from the bedroom at Castle Dracula, including the diary, which HESLING picks up.

     HESLING
  (distorted voice) On the floor, I discovered
  a silver portrait frame. The glass was shattered
  and the portrait had been ripped out....a torn
  piece still remained in one corner.....

There is a discreet knock at the door.

     HESLING:
  Well?

HESLING crosses to the machine and switches it off, as the door opens to reveal an UNDER MANAGER. He glances nervously at the recording machine.

     UNDER MANAGER
  A thousand apologies for disturbing you,
  Doctor Van Hesling...it is necessary to ascertain
  when you consider you will be vacating this suite
  of rooms....other clients, you understand

         (46 - 47)

INT. HESLING'S HOTEL SUITE. NIGHT.   (Cont'd)

        HESLING:
I don't know yet...possibly tomorrow.....
possibly not. (dismissing him) I'll let
you know.

        UNDER MANAGER:
The manager would consider it a personal favour
if you would give him as much notice as....

        HESLING:
(firmly) I said I'll let you know. Goodnight.

        UNDERMANAGER:
(he isn't sure whether he has made his point
or not) Er - goodnight, doctor.

With a final glance at the 'infernal machine'. he retreats.

HESLING moves back to the Dictaphone and, lifting the needle, drops it back a couple of grooves. He switches on again. The voice grinds up to speed.

        HESLING:
(voice distort) ..the glass was shattered and
the portrait had been ripped out....a torn piece
still remained in one corner...

HESLING is looking thoughtfully at the frame.

        HESLING:
(voice distort) Whose portrait was it? Was it
that of Jonathon's fiancee, Lucy?...if so, why
had Dracula taken it?.....What could he have
wanted with it?

        CUT OR MIX:

48. <u>INT. LUCY'S BEDROOM. NIGHT</u>

LUCY is still laying on top of the bedclothes with her head turned towards the French Windows, where the curtains are moving restlessly in the night breeze.

Then across the window there passes a fleeting shadow.

C.S. LUCY

She stiffens momentarily, then relaxes again, waiting.

C.S. DRACULA

He is standing just inside the French Windows.

(47 - 48)

40.

INT. LUCY'S BEDROOM. NIGHT. (Cont'd)

C.S. DRACULA

He is dressed as when we last saw him, in complete unrelieved black, with his long high collared cloak.

His eyes are blazing in his head with hypnotic intensity.

Then he smiles a tight little smile that reels back his upper lip exposing his two canine teeth.

C.S. LUCY

Expressionless, waiting.

C.S. DRACULA

Slowly he starts towards her as we:

> DISSOLVE:

49 INT. HALL. DAY.

GERDA the housekeeper is just opening the door to disclose a fat and rather pompous DOCTOR SEWARD.

GERDA looks very upset.

> SEWARD:
> Morning.

> MINA:
> (voice) Is that the doctor?

> GERDA:
> Yes Ma'am.

They turn as MINA comes from LUCY'S room.

> MINA:
> Good morning Doctor Seward.....I'm so glad you could come.

SEWARD is removing his cloak.

> SEWARD
> I came as soon as I got your message my dear. What seems to be the trouble this morning?

> MINA:
> She's worse Doctor.....much worse.

(48 - 49)

INT. HALL. DAY (Cont'd)

GERDA looks as if she might burst into tears.

          SEWARD:
I see, well it's no more than I expected.

          MINA:
That'll be all for the moment Gerda.

          GERDA:
Yes'm...

She bobs a curtsy, and with a final sniff she leaves.

MINA turns to the DOCTOR as she starts leading him towards LUCY'S room.

          MINA:
Poor Gerda, she does love Lucy so, she can't bear that she should be ill.

          DOCTOR:
These domestics are all the same my hear. They form personal attachments to those they work for.

          MINA:
Oh I don't think there's anything un-healthy in the way Gerda feels. She has a little girl you know....Lucy is very good to her.

          DOCTOR:
Be that as it may my dear, domestic's place is in the kitchen....shall we go in.

They are outside LUCY'S door.

          MINA:
Of course.

MINA opens the door and she goes in followed by SEWARD.

50.   INT. LUCY'S ROOM. DAY.

LUCY is lying in bed. She looks like death, as though most of the blood has been drained from her body, which in fact it has been. She is in some sort of a coma, and she doesn't move or open her eyes as the two of them move in, one either side of the bed.

SEWARD picks up her limp wrist and starts to take her pulse.

          MINA:
She was like this this morning when I came in to wake her. She hasn't stirred.

(49 - 50)

INT. LUCY'S ROOM. DAY. (Cont'd)

          SEWARD:
Hmph.

He hangs on to the wrist for a couple more seconds, then drops it. He leans over LUCY and lifts one of her eye lids and peers into her eyes.

Then he straightens up. MINA looks at him.

          SEWARD:
Hmph.

          MINA:
What is it Doctor?

          SEWARD:
It's difficult to put into words that the laymen....

He smiles

.....laywomen, would understand I'm afraid.

          MINA:
Can't you tell me anything?

          SEWARD:
It's......it's a rare form of anaemia....that's what's sapping her strength.

          MINA:
What about those marks on her neck?

          SEWARD:
What marks?

          MINA:
There....look.

SEWARD looks, then looks again, more closely. Then he straightens up again.

          SEWARD:
They've got nothing to do with her condition, anything at all.

          MINA:
Then what are they?

          SEWARD:
Just some form of sting....mesquito probably...

He turns from the bed and starts toward the door.

INT LUCY'S ROOM. DAY. (Cont'd)

          SEWARD:
Keep on with the treatments as I have prescribed.

          MINA:
It has done very little good.

          SEWARD
Please.....allow me to be the judge of that.

He looks at MINA pompously for a moment, and finally MINA nods.

          MINA:
Very well doctor....I'll show you out.

She opens the door for SEWARD and they go into the hall.

51. <u>INT. HALL. DAY.</u>

Just as MINA and SEWARD come from LUCY's room, a little girl about seven comes running from the door that leads to the kitchen. This is VERA, GERDA'S daughter.
She goes straight to MINA.

          VERA:
May I go and see Aunt Lucy now?

          SEWARD:
No child you can't.

VERA looks towards him.

          VERA:
Why not?

          MINA:
Aunt Lucy is sick.

VERA looks back at MINA.

          VERA:
What's the matter with her?

          MINA:
She's.....she's just not very well.

She turns back to SEWARD.

          VERA:
Don't you know what's wrong with her?

          SEWARD:
Of course I do child.

(50 - 51)

44.

INT. HALL. DAY. (Cont'd)

> VERA:
> Then why don't you make her better?

> MINA:
> Hush Vera

> VERA:
> Well why doesn't he, he's the doctor. My mummy says he's......

> MINA:
> Vera. We don't want to know what Mummy says. Now run along, there's a good girl.

> GERDA:
> (off) Vera....where are you?

They turn as GERDA comes from the kitchen.

> GERDA:
> How many times have I told you child that you mustn't go bothering Mrs. Holmwood.

> VERA:
> I only wanted to see Auntey Lucy.

> GERDA:
> Well you can't......now come back to the kitchen. I'm sorry Ma'am.

> MINA:
> Tat's alright Gerda.

She smiles as VERA runs off, then rejoins the DOCTOR who has donned his cloak.

> SEWARD:
> I shall be round again tomorrow. Until then, remember, plenty of fresh air....you might even try leaving the garden doors open tonight. We'll soon blow the grims out of her system eh....

He turns to the door and opens it.

> bye my dear.....and don't worry.

> MINA:
> Good bye Doctor.

She closes the door behind her, looking as though she has every intention of worrying.

DISSOLVE:
(51)

52. INT. HESLING'S HOTEL SUITE. DAY.

The room is empty. On the table, JONATHON'S possessions have been tied into a neat bundle.

There is a knock at the door.

> HESLING:
> (voice) Come in.

The outer door opens to reveal MINA. She stands on the threshold, not liking to come in.

> HESLING:
> (voice) I'm so glad you could come, Miss Lucy I just......

The bedroom door has opened and HELSING enters.
He stops dead when he sees MINA . There is an awkward silence.

> MINA:
> (embarrassed) Good morning.

> HESLING:
> Good morning, Mrs. Holmwood. Won't you come in?

As he ushers her in, he glares at an unopened letter which MINA carries in her gloved hand. He takes it from her.

> HESLING:
> I see that the note I sent Miss Lucy was intercepted....by your husband?

> MINA:
> No, it was I.

> HESLING:
> No matter. It was simply that I wanted Miss Lucy to have these. They were Jonathon's.

He indicates the bundle.

> MINA:
> I have to explain, doctor, that Lucy is sick.
> We have not told her yet.

> HESLING:
> I see, well, I wisher her a speedy recovery, in the meanwhile, perhaps you would be good enough to...

He has picked up the silver picture frame. Suddenly, he realises the implication of what MINA has just said. He turns to her.

(52)

INT. HESLING'S HOTEL SUITE. DAY. (Cont'd)

          HESLING:
How long has she been sick?

          MINA:
A few days....Doctor Seward says it is a some form of anaemia, but.....

          HELSING:
(urgently) I must see Miss Lucy....Immediately... and this time you husband must not stop me....

          MIX TO:

53. INT. LUCY'S ROOM. DAY.

LUCY is laying on her back with her hand turned away from CAMERA so that the mark on her neck is not visible.

After a moment a hand comes into picture and shakes her gently by the shoulder.

As her eyes open, CAMERA eases back to disclose MINA, who is shaking her awake, and VAN HESLING standing behind her.

          MINA:
Lucy dear.....I've brought someone to see you.

LUCY takes a second to orientate herself. When she speaks her voice is faint and quite without expression.

          LUCY:
Hello Mina....I was asleep.

          MINA:
I know dear.

          LUCY:
Who's this?

          MINA:
This is a Dr. Van Hesling....he was....he's a friend of Jonathon's.

          LUCY:
Jonathon's dead, isn't he?

MINA and HESLING exchange quick glances.

          LUCY:
He is isn't he?

          (52 - 53)

INT LUCY'S ROOM. DAY. (Cont'd)

She is rather matter of fact about the whole thing.

Finally MINA nods.

      LUCY:
  I knew that he was.

      MINA:
  Darling, who told you was it Arthur?

LUCY shakes her head.

      MINA:
  Who then?

LUCY looks at her.

      LUCY:
  Nobody told me....I just knew that's all. Is
  that why Dr. Van Hesling is here?

      MINA:
  Partly...but how did you.....?

      LUCY:
  I'm sorry you've had a wasted journey, sir.

VAN HESLING smiles.

      HESLING:
  Not at all...I understand that you are not well.

      LUCY:
  That's what they say.

      HESLING:
  (gently) Do you mind if I just have a look at
  your neck?

LUCY flashes him a glance of suspicion. Her hand automatically goes to her neck to cover the marks.

      HESLING:
  It's quite alright, I won't hurt you.

Gently but quite firmly he pulls LUCY'S hand away from her neck until he can quite clearly see the marks of the vampire.

      MINA:
  Doctor Seward said they were some sort of a
  sting....a bite of some sort

HESLING straightens up slowly.

      HESLING
  When did they first appear?   (53)

INT. LUCY'S ROOM. DAY. (Cont'd)

          MINA:
When she was first taken ill.

HESLING stands for a moment, then he turns to MINA.

          HESLING:
Please will you show me out?

MINA looks at him a little surprised at his abruptness.

          MINA:
Of course.

He bows perfunctorily to LUCY who stares back at him, then he starts for the door, MINA follows.

54. **INT. HALL. DAY.**

HESLING come out of LUCY'S room, followed by MINA. As MINA closes the door behind her she sees HESLING deep in thought. Then HESLING looks up.

          HESLING:
Are you sure that she could not have known about the death of Jonathon Harker?

          MINA:
Quite sure, I cannot understand it....and she is taking it so well....it, it frightens me.

          HESLING:
You have cause to be frightened. Now I would like to try something...something that may make her well again.

          MINA:
Oh if only you could....anything.

          HESLING:
(riding) I'm not promising anything, but if you do what I say, I shall know in the morning whether my suspicions are correct. If they are then perhaps we can think of some way to further the cure.

          MINA:
What is it that you want me to do?

          HESLING:
First I want some garlic....I want the bulbs and the flowers. Do you know where I can get any?

          MINA:
Here...we have a profusion of it in the garden.

(53-54)

INT. HALL. DAY. (Cont'd)

          HESLING:
Good. Now I want you to pick as many flowers of this plant as possible and put them in vases. These vases you will stand around in Miss Lucy's room....

MINA starts to say something.

....let me finish. Then you will take some bulbs of garlic and slice them. These you will rub along the frames of the doors and the windows of the room. Seal the room with garlic if you can understand what I mean.

          MINA:
I can understand your actions, but for the life of me I cannot see what your motives may be.

          HESLING:
One other thing....the windows and the doors in Miss Lucy's room must be kept tight shut from dusk to dawn.

          MINA:
But Doctor Seward left instructions to the contrary...

Suddenly HESLING blazes....not with rage so much a righteous indignation that such a thing should be happening.

          HESLING:
I do not care what this Doctor Seward said. Do what I have told you, and we may be able to save the young girl in there. Do not do it, and she will die as sure as I am standing here.

On MINA'S horrified look we:

          DISSOLVE:

55. **INT. HALL. NIGHT**

MINA comes up from the kitchen carrying a vase of garlic flowers, which she carries into LUCY'S room.

56. **INT. LUCY'S ROOM. NIGHT**

LUCY is laying back in bed. She doesn't seem as composed as when we last saw her, rather is she restless, tossing from side to side on the bed.

She looks up as MINA comes in with another vase to join the five or six that are already placed at various points around the room.

(54 - 56)

INT. LUCY'S ROOM. NIGHT. (Cont'd)

> LUCY:
> Why Mina....why?

> MINA:
> Never you mind. Dr. Van Hesling is a very clever man....Dr. Seward hasn't seemed to be able to do any good, we'll see what happens now.

> LUCY:
> But they smell....they smell terrible.

> MINA:
> That's probably why he suggested them. You've been bitten by something....the garlic is to keep it out of the room. That's why we're having the windows shut as well.

LUCY subsides weakly onto her pillow again.

> LUCY:
> If you say so Mina...

> MINA:
> I do say so...now you try and get some sleep. Are you sure you don't mind Arthur and I going out?

> LUCY:
> Of course not....these business dinners are so important to Arthur.

MINA bends down and kisses LUCY on the forehead.

> MINA:
> Good night my dear.

> LUCY:
> Good night Mina.

MINA takes up the lamp and gets to the door. She looks back at LUCY once more from the door, then she goes out.

57. INT. HALL. NIGHT.

ARTHUR is just getting into his cloak and hat. He turns when he sees MINA.

> ARTHUR:
> Hurry my dear...we don't want to be late.

> MINA:
> I am ready, except for my cloak...

(56 - 57)

INT. HALL. NIGHT. (Cont'd)

She looks up as GERDA comes downstairs carrying MINA'S cloak.

She holds it up for MINA to put on.

                    MINA:
Thank you Gerda...we won't be too late.

                    GERDA:
Away with you both and have a good time. And don't worry about Miss Lucy. I'll watch over her.

MINA smiles her thanks.

ARTHUR has moved over to the front door and is holding it open for MINA.

MINA, followed by GERDA comes to the door and goes out.

                    ARTHUR:
Good night Gerda.

                    GERDA:
Good night sir.

ARTHUR goes out, and GERDA hangs on to the front door watching them for a moment to see that they get off safely.

The she comes in and shuts the door behind her.

She turns and starts for the kitchen. She is just about to go through when she has an afterthought, and she moves over to the door to LUCY'S room instead.

She stops for a moment with her ear pressed up to the door, listening.

Then she moves back in the direction of the kitchen.

                    DISSOLVE:

58.   INT. LUCY'S ROOM. NIGHT.

Start on a vase of garlic flowers and pan across to LUCY.

She is tossing and turning in bed in some sort of a daze.

C.S. LUCY.

Suddenly her eyes snap open and she lays for a moment unable to orientate herself.

Then she rolls her head sideways and looks towards the French Windows.

(56 - 58)

INT. LUCY'S ROOM. NIGHT. (Cont'd)

C.S. FRENCH WINDOWS

They are shut tight and a vase of garlic flowers is standing on each sill either side of the door.

C.S. LUCY

Her face wrinkles up in an expression half of distaste, which changes to one of loathing.

She struggles to a sitting position, stares at the flowers as if hypnotised. Then suddenly, she calls out....

>   LUCY:
> (calling) Mina......Mina....

She looks round her again.

C.S. VASE OF FLOWERS

Standing on her bedside table.

C.S. LUCY

Suddenly she can stand it no more.

>   LUCY:
> (calling) Mina......

She sweeps her hand round and knocks the vase by the bedside flying.

It hits the floor and shatters.

C.S. DOOR.

At the same time the door opens and GERDA comes in. She sees the shattered vase and LUCY sitting up in bed.

>   GERDA:
> Heavens child.....what is it....

M.S.

She hurries over to the edge of the bed.

>   LUCY:
> Oh Gerda.....these flowers.....I can't stand them...

GERDA looks around her sniffing.

>   GERDA:
> They are strong aren't they.....but Mrs. Holmwood said that...

(58)

INT. LUCY'S ROOM. (Cont'd)

> LUCY:
> I don't care what she said Gerda...you must take them out.....please....please...

C.S. GERDA

She stands there for a moment wondering what to do.

C.S. LUCY

She is looking pleadingly at GERDA:

> LUCY:
> Please Gerda....they make me feel so ill

M.S.

Suddenly GERDA makes up her mind.

> GERDA:
> Alright Miss Lucy....I'll take them out.

She moves over to one of the vases and picks it up.

> LUCY:
> And the windows Gerda....you'll open the windows.....

> GERDA:
> Yes Miss if that's what you want.

She goes out with the vase leaving the door open.

C.S. LUCY

She lies down in the bed again, then she rolls her head in the direction of the French Windows.

There is something almost like a smile at the corner of her mouth.

> DISSOLVE:

59. INT. LUCY'S ROOM. DAY

We start on a close shot of LUCY, showing plainly the two marks on her throat.

She is still with the stillness of death.

After a moment CAMERA starts to pull back at the same time as a sheet is pulled up over her face.

(58 - 59)

INT. LUCY'S ROOM. DAY. (Cont'd)

We can hear muffled sobs from out of picture, and as we get further back we see it is MINA.

Also in the room are SEWARD, who has covered LUCY up and ARTHUR.

SEWARD turns from the bed and looks at ARTHUR.

> SEWARD
> ......There was nothing I could do.

ARTHUR says nothing. He moves over to MINA and puts his arm around her as SEWARD moves across towards the window. Then they all turn as there is a knock on the door.

It opens to disclose GERDA. She too has been crying, now she looks apologetic.

> GERDA:
> I'm sorry sir...there's a Mr. Van Hesling.....
> he insists on seeing you....

ARTHUR seems almost unable to believe his ears for a moment then he steps forward.

> ARTHUR:
> He insists does he.....I'll tell....

He gets no further. The door is pushed wide open from behind GERDA and HESLING strides in past her.

> HESLING:
> Is it true what this woman tells me?

He looks round, then his gaze fixes on the figure of LUCY under the bedclothes.

He strides over to the bed quickly and lifts the sheet from her face.

Then he lets the sheet fall back. He turns to the others livid.

> HESLING:
> Well?

They all look at him as though he is mad.

> HESLING:
> Who is responsible for this?

Finally ARTHUR steps forward.

> ARTHUR:
> This is your doing Hesling. YOU are responsible.

(59)

INT. LUCY'S ROOM. DAY. (Cont'd)

          HESLING:
(gently) Mrs. Holmwood....did you do as I told you?

          SEWARD:
She did...and that is the reason the poor child has been taken from us.

          HESLING:
(coldly) You are doctor Seward?

          SEWARD:
I am, and I.....

          HESLING:
Well Doctor.....are you proud of your work?

          SEWARD:
What do you mean sir?

          HESLING:
This girl here....this dead girl.

SEWARD become almost apoplectic.

          SEWARD:
I've heard of you Hesling....you're an important man....a clever man it's been said. But by what right did you assume the responsibility of deciding what was best for my patient.....especially in view of the fact that it was completely opposite to the treatment I prescribed....tell me that sir.

HESLING looks at him steadily.

          HESLING:
For what were you treating her Doctor?

This is a bit of a setback for SEWARD, but he rallies after a beat.

          SEWARD:
Mrs. Holmwood here informs me that acting under you instructions she filled this room with evil smelling flowers and shut....

          HESLING:
I know what my instructions were.....

          SEWARD:
Then you know that she died as a direct result of what you ordered Mrs. Holmwood to do.

INT. LUCY'S ROOM. DAY. (Cont'd)

        HESLING:
I know nothing of the sort.

        SEWARD:
The room was sealed up with all the windows and doors shut tight....it's no wonder the poor child died....even had she been a person of normal health she would have probably suffered the same fate.

He turns to ARTHUR.

        HESLING:
You believe him?

        ARTHUR:
I do...and I will ask you to leave this house.

Ignoring him and SEWARD, HESLING moves over so that he is looking down at MINA.

        HESLING:
(gently) Mrs. Holmwood. I can only hope that through your grief you can see sufficiently clearly to recognise that what I did had nothing.......nothing to do with the death of your husbands' sister. Rather, blame the person who took the flowers from this room after they had been placed here.

MINA looks up for the first time.

        MINA:
How.....how did you know they were taken out?

        HESLING:
If they had not have been, then Miss Lucy would still be alive.

C.S. ARTHUR AND SEWARD

They look at one another for a moment as we:

        DISSOLVE:

60.   EXT. GRAVEYARD. STUDIO. DAY.

This is two days later.

A coffin is being carried from the chapel in the background towards the mausoleum that is to be LUCY'S tomb.

        (59 - 60)

EXT. GRAVEYARD. DAY. (Cont'd)

Behind the coffin move ARTHUR and MINA, then GERDA, then a couple of unidentifiable relatives. All the ladies are heavily veiled.

The procession, headed by a priest, moves toward the tomb, then at the door, the priest stands aside and allows the coffin to be carried past him into the tomb.

Then into big foreground steps the figure of VAN HESLING, so that we are shooting across his back towards the tomb in the b.g.

After a couple of moments the coffin bearers come from the tomb, and the priest signals to a locksmith or somesuch who is standing nearby to lock the tomb up.

Then he turns and says something to ARTHUR and MINA, and starts to walk away.

ARTHUR and MINA turn and start to walk towards where HESLING is standing, and in foreground HESLING moves in preparation to meeting them.

MINA sees him before ARTHUR and her step falters. ARTHUR, who has his arm around her looks to see what caused it, and recognises HESLING.

He looks over his shoulder and beckons GERDA closer with his head.

To GERDA he hands over MINA, then he steps out towards HESLING, who stands waiting for him.

TWO SHOT

HESLING is waiting and after a second ARTHUR steps into frame. He is livid.

          ARTHUR
Have you shred of decency left?

HESLING holds up his head.

          HESLING:
One moment. I have come here to give you this. When you have read it, you may come to my hotel suite and insult me until you exhaust yourself if you so desire. Until then, I shall ask you to hold your peace. Good day.

He hands ARTHUR something, tips his hat, turns and walks off.

ARTHUR watches after him for a moment then looks down at what he has in his hand.

(60)

EXT. GRAVEYARD. DAY. (Cont'd)

INSERT

It is the diary.

ARTHUR flips over the title page and we read the words:

                The Diary of Jonathon Harker.

And we:

                              FADE OUT.

FADE IN:

61. INT. SITTING ROOM. NIGHT.

C.S. GERDA

She is standing in the door looking past CAMERA. She looks scared.

> GERDA:
> It's the police sir....they want to see you.

M.S.

ARTHUR and MINA are seated either side of the fireplace.

> MINA:
> What's it about Gerda?

> GERDA:
> I don't ma'am....I'm sorry ma'am...but they've got Vera with them.

> MINA:
> There's nothing wrong with her is there Gerda?

> GERDA:
> I don't know Ma'am.....just that they've got her with them and they want to see you....ooh wait till I get that child alone.

> MINA:
> You'd better show them in Gerda.

> GERDA:
> Very good ma'am.

She does an about face and we hear her from the hall.

> GERDA:
> (outside) Will you come this way please.....not you Vera....I want to talk to you.

> VOICE:
> (outside) I want the little girl for a few moments if you don't mind.

Then the door opens to admit a very large plain clothed policeman. He is holding by the hand VERA, GERDA'S little girl, who's looking rather worried about the whole thing.

> POLICEMAN:
> Evening M'm....evening sir.

> ARTHUR:
> What can we do for you officer.

(61)

INT. SITTING ROOM. NIGHT. (Cont'd)

          POLICEMAN:
I'm not rightly sure sir as yet....we'll see.

He turns to the little girl.

          POLICEMAN:
Tell them what you told me.

VERA looks around fearfully.

          MINA:
It's alright darling, don't be frightened.

          VERA:
I was out by myself....she came up to me.....
she said hello Vera...shall we go for a little
walk....I said yes and we walked a little way
and she said shall we sit down and I said yes...
then she went to kiss me....but someone came
along and she got up and ran away.

          GERDA:
Who did dear .....who was she?

C.S. VERA

          VERA:
Aunt Lucy

C.S. MINA

Reaction

C.S. ARTHUR

His reaction in infinitely more terrible than MINA'S

M.S.

          POLICEMAN:
Now I would like to speak to the 'Aunt Lucy' if you
don't mind.....there are one or two questions that
must be answered.

There is a long silence from everybody.

          POLICEMAN:
You understand that this could be serious....
enticement of a juvenile is a nasty business...
very nasty.....

Still no-one says anything. Finally ARTHUR steps forward.

(61)

61.

INT. SITTING ROOM. NIGHT. (Cont'd)

      ARTHUR:
  Lucy Holmwood was my sister officer.

      POLICEMAN:
  Then perhaps you'll ask....WAS you sister?

      ARTHUR:
  She died three days ago.

          DISSOLVE:

62. <u>EXT. GRAVEYARD. STUDIO. NIGHT.</u>

This is the graveyard where LUCY was buried. Indeed the featured part of the set up is LUCY'S tomb, standing out gaunt and mysterious in the moonlight.

After a moment ARTHUR steps into the foreground, looking towards the tomb.

Then he starts towards it.

C.S. AT TOMB

After a moment ARTHUR comes into frame, slowly and hesitatingly.

He moves to the door of the tomb, and lifting his hand he places it gently on the door.

It opens inwards at a touch.

He stands where he is for a second, then pulling himself together, he ducks his head and steps through the door.

63. <u>INT. TOMB. NIGHT.</u>

In the centre of the tomb is a raised plinth. On the plinth is a coffin, a new coffin with the brass work still gleaming.

ARTHUR comes in through the door, hesitates, then starts towards the coffin.

He reaches it and puts out a hand to touch the brass plate set in the lid.

INSERT.

The plate reads

       LUCY HOLMWOOD 1875 - 1899

           (61 - 63)

INT. TOMB. NIGHT.   (Cont'd)

C.S. ARTHUR

He lifts his hand from the plate and gets a grip on the underside of the lid of the coffin. Then he hesitates, afraid to look.

Finally, he plucks up enough courage and throws back the lid of the coffin.

C.S. COFFIN

The coffin is empty.

C.S. ARTHUR

He looks as if he might pass right out.

DISSOLVE TO:

64. INT SERVANT'S BEDROOM. STUDIO. NIGHT.

In her iron bedstand, GERDA sleeps heavily muttering and grunting as she dreams.

The little cot near the window is empty, the bedclothes thrown back.

65. EXT. WOODS. STUDIO. NIGHT. - EXT. LOT

Wending her way along a narrow path through the undergrowth is VERA dressed in her nightgown.

Her eyes are glazed and she walks as if listening for something, turning her head from side to side.

AS she approaches camera, she stops - looks up past us.

    VERA:
 Did you call me, Aunt Lucy?

C.S. LUCY

This is a different LUCY. She seems more voluptuous, more wanton.

Her hair has matted slightly and her face is slightly streaked with dirt.

But the most noticeable change about her is the fact that her two canine teeth have grown enormously an they now slightly overlap her lower lip.

She smiles at VERA, a terrifying smile.

(63 - 65)

EXT. WOODS. STUDIO. NIGHT. (Cont'd)

       LUCY:
  Yes, darling......

LUCY hold out a hand.

       LUCY:
  Come...

       VERA:
  Where are we going....?

She takes LUCY'S hand.

  .....you're cold...

       LUCY:
  We'll go for a little walk....I know somewhere
  nice and quiet where we can.....play.

She starts off through the buses, and VERA with her hand in LUCY'S follows obediently.

As they get further away, there is a sudden agitating of the bushes close to camera, and into foreground steps the figure of a man.

We can only see him from the neck down, but sufficient that he is wearing black clothes and a long cloak.

He watches after the figure of LUCY and VERA for a moment as we

       SOFT WIPE TO:

66. <u>EXT. GRAVEYARD. STUDIO. NIGHT</u>

ARTHUR is standing a little way from the tomb, where he can see the door.

He is waiting. Suddenly he stiffens into watchfulness.

L.S.

Through the tombstones come two shadowy figures. It is difficult to make them out at first, then as they draw closer we see that they are LUCY and VERA.

       VERA:
  Is it much further, Aunt Lucy?

       LUCY:
  Nearly there, my darling.

64.

EXT. GRAVEYARD. STUDIO. NIGHT. (Cont'd)

After a pause.

      VERA:
  Aunt Lucy, my neck is sore.

      LUCY:
  I'll kiss it better in a moment, my darling.

LUCY starts to lad VERA towards the open door of the tomb, when suddenly she whirls round at the sound of a voice.

      ARTHUR:
  (Off) Lucy.....

C.S. ARTHUR

He has moved forward, not wishing to believe what he can see.

LUCY lets go of VERA'S hand as she recognises ARTHUR. We see here that she's already been at VERA, her chin and front of her gown being spotted with blood.

She smiles when she sees ARTHUR, a diabolical smile of welcome.

      LUCY:
  Arthur....my dear brother...

She steps forward towards him.

M.S.

      ARTHUR:
  Lucy.....I....

LUCY continues her advance.

      LUCY:
  Dear Arthur....why didn't you come sooner...

Her arms are stretched towards him.

  ....come, let me kiss you.

ARTHUR stands rooted to the spot, unable to move at the horror of what confronts him.

Then LUCY reaches him and puts her hands on his shoulders.

Then suddenly there is a flash of light and between the two figures is pushed an arm holding a crucifix. It is VAN HESLING.

           (66)

EXT. GRAVEYARD. STUDIO. NIGHT (Cont'd)

He presses the crucifix in the centre of LUCY's forehead.

C.S. LUCY

She screams in agony, and as she jumps back from the crucifix we see burned into her forehead, a livid red weal.

She looks towards HESLING and ARTHUR for a moment, almost gnashing her teeth.

WHO SHOT HESLING AND ARTHUR

They are standing together looking at her. ARTHUR still sick with horror.

Finally LUCY turns and runs quickly into the tomb.

HESLING stands for a moment, then he goes over to where VERA has been watching wide eyed with fear. He goes down on one knee beside her.

> HESLING:
> Would you like me to take you home?

VERA nods her head.

> HESLING
> Wait here while I fetch the other gentleman and we'll walk home together.

> VERA:
> (urgently) Not Aunt Lucy

> HESLING:
> No, not Aunt Lucy.....look over there, if you watch you'll see the day beginning.

VERA turns her eyes towards where HESLING is pointing. HESLING gets to his feet and after looking at her for a beat he starts into the tomb.

C.S. INTO COFFIN

LUCY'S eyes are closed. The blood still smears her chin.

EXT. GRAVEYARD. STUDIO. NIGHT. (Cont'd)

WIDER SHOT

ARTHUR stares down into the tomb, his face drawn and pale.

VAN HESLING joins him.

> HESLING:
> (quietly but coldly) You are now witness to the filth and degradation of this vampire Dracula that Jonathon Harker died trying to destroy. I am sorry that your sister should be the victim.

ARTHUR looks up at HESLING steadily.

> ARTHUR:
> That is not my sister.

> HESLING:
> No. This is not your Lucy. This is just a shell possessed with the evil of her bestial master (becoming excited). But she can be his downfall. Sooner or later she must lead us to him. Then, pray God we shall be able to destroy his cult of evil for all time. Ever since Lucy became one of the damned - The Undead, I have been watching her. This is the first time she has ventured abroad at night. She must go to him soon...she must.

> ARTHUR:
> (shouts) No! (quieter) no, she must not remain like this.....she must regain her soul. There is a way.....you know there is.

> HESLING:
> Not yet....not yet....she is our only hope of reaching him.

> ARTHUR:
> What about that child out there? And the others she will defile? No! she must be freed of this horror. I demand it. I have the right.

HESLING stares at ARTHUR for a moment.

> HESLING:
> You know how it must be done?

> ARTHUR
> I have read Jonathon's diary.

(66)

EXT. GRAVEYARD. STUDIO. NIGHT. (Cont'd)

There is a long pause, finally HESLING speaks again.

> HESLING:
> Very well then. Take the child home, I will meet you hear in an hour.

DISSOLVE:

67. INT. TOMB. NIGHT.

Start on a canvas holdall being unrolled exposing the needle sharp stake and the mallet.

PULL back as a hand comes in and takes up a stake and the mallet, to see HESLING start towards the open coffin.

ARTHUR is watching him. Then ARTHUR steps forward and holds out his hand.

> ARTHUR:
> I will do it....it is my responsibility.....and it is my fault that it happened.

HESLING looks at him for a moment, then holds out the mallet and stake which ARTHUR takes.

Then he moves towards the open coffin, HESLING just behind him.

He stops for a moment looking down into the coffin. Then he reaches forward.

C.S. LUCY

The hand comes in holding the sharpened stake. The point is laid just below her left breast, forming a slight indentation in the body of the girl.

C.S. ARTHUR

He raises the mallet, then looks sideways at HESLING.

C.S. HELSING

He is looking at ARTHUR. He nods.

C.S. ARTHUR

He brings the mallet hown hard on the head of the stake.

(66 - 67)

INT. TOMB. (Cont'd)

C.S. LUCY

Three things happen simultaneously.

The steak sinks deep into her breast, and blood starts welling out. Her eyes snap open suddenly, turning on the two men. And she screams, a long drawn out animal scream of pain.

Then as the mallet crashes down on the head of the stake again driving it further in, she starts to struggle to escape from the stake that is embedded in her.

She writhes and twists, all the time screaming, while the blood flows up around the edge of the stake staining her white clothing a bright wet red.

C.S. ARTHUR

He manages one more clout with the mallet, then he drops back from the coffin, releasing his hold on the stake.

TWO SHOT

Quickly HELSING takes the mallet from his slack hand, and turning to the coffin he gives the stake another clout.

C.S. LUCY

The stake is now almost completely embedded in her chest, and her movements are growing less. The screams begin to die down to a whimper.

C.S. HESLING

He hits the stake once more, then stands back.

C.S. ARTHUR

Almost physically sick at what he has done. After a moment, when all is quiet, HESLING'S hand touches him gently on the shoulder.

TWO SHOT

HESLING indicates for him to look into the coffin.

Steeling himself ARTHUR steps forward and peers into the coffin.

C.S. LUCY

In spite of the blood that is all about her LUCY looks different, she looks at peace.

INT. TOMB. (Cont'd)

C.S. LUCY

Her eyes are closed, the wantonness is gone from her face, and even the canine teeth are no longer visible. Instead, around her mouth is the faintest trace of a smile, a gentle smile of rest.

DISSOLVE:

68. INT. HESLING'S HOTEL SUITE. DAY.

It is an hour or so later.

VAN HESLING is pouring out a very large neat brandy, which he carries across to ARTHUR, who is looking very upset after his terrifying experience.

HESLING hands ARTHUR the drink, which he downs in two long draughts. He grimaces as he hands back the empty glass.

          ARTHUR:
Thank you.

HESLING carries the drink back to the table. He is deep in thought.

          ARTHUR
What...now?

HESLING turns slowly from the table.

          HESLING:
Lucy was my only lead to Dracula....eventually she would have been bound to go to him.

          ARTHUR:
I had to do it.

          HESLING:
Of course.

          ARTHUR:
Just as I'll do anything to help you find this....fiend.

          HESLING:
(thoughtfully) If you are to help me...

          ARTHUR:
I'll do anything you say.

(67 - 68)

INT. HESLING'S HOTEL SUITE. DAY. (Cont'd)

          HESLING:
Good. But if you are to help me you must have some protection - the protection of knowledge. I am going to tell you the truth about vamprism - a synthesis of yours of study and research.... of sifting truth from superstition; fact from fiction. It embraces the lore and experience of the Ancients as well as others who, like myself, have studied the powers of the Un-dead.

He ponders for a moment, then starts his exposition.

          HESLING:

The popular conception that the vampire is able to turn itself into a bat or wolf or any form of animal life is nonsense. The vampire is as rigidly bound by the natural laws of flesh and blood as you or I....with one important exception. A vampire cannot die he is cursed with immortality - he must go on age after age adding new victims to this unholy cult, who, in their turn, become Un-dead. Two things, and two things only can destroy a vampire - the first you have witnessed tonight; the second is exposure to the light of the sun; a vampire cannot tolerate the day light, even indirectly.

ARTHUR is staring at him, aghast. He can hardly believe his ears.

          ARTHUR:
You mean that Lucy could have regained her soul by simply exposing her to the rays of the sun....and yet you let me drive a stake through her body.

          HESLING:
Restrain yourself for one moment. I said that vampires could be destroyed by exposure to the sun - they cannot regain their souls that way. What you did was the only way. You have released her soul.....given her peace.

ARTHUR subsides, scratching his head in bewilderment. This is all too much for him.

          ARTHUR:
I'm sorry. Please...

          HESLING:
If neither of these two things happen to a vampire, he will live on for ever, replenishing his body during the hours of darkness with the warm blood of living humans.

(68)

INT HESLING'S HOTEL SUITE. DAY.

ARTHUR:
You mean this dracula could be....hundreds of years old.

HESLING:
There is evidence of the existence of a Count Dracula more than six hundred years ago. Of course, he could be an antecedent of the present Dracula, but it is my belief he is the same person. (urgently) That is why he must be destroyed. If we allow him to escape us, he will be free to spread his reign of sickening horror for another six hundred years.

ARTHUR:
How do we even start to look for him? He could be anywhere. now.....his own home...

HESLING:
(shakes head) He will be here, close to us, waiting for Lucy to come to him.

ARTHUR:
But why did he pick here? Why Lucy?

HESLING:
For revenge....revenge against Jonathon for what he did to his woman. When Lucy had become versed in the ways of her new existence, he would have taken her home with him...to replace the woman that Jonathon had destroyed.

ARTHUR:
I see.

HESLING:
(thoughtfully) The day I visited the House of Dracula, to search for Jonathon, a large hearse drove out of the grounds carrying a coffin. During the hours of daylight a vampire has to return to his native soil.

ARTHUR:
That coffin could have contained soil.....

HESLING:
To reach here it would have to cross the border at Ingstadt. Crossing frontiers, one has to comply with certain formalities.

INT. HESLING'S HOTEL SUITE. DAY. (Cont'd)

He moves over to a bell-pull and jerks it violently.

> HESLING:
> We must go there....now!

> HESLING:
> We'll take my coach.....twelve hours should see us there....every moment increases the chance for him to select another victim now that Lucy is denied him. We must do all in our power to forestall him.

A SERVANT appears in the doorway.

> HESLING:
> (barks it out) My coach......immediately.

The SERVANT scuttles away.

> HESLING:
> If we do not forestall him, the God protect the unfortunate creature whom Dracula selects for his nest victim.

> MIX TO:

69. INT. SITTING ROOM. NIGHT.

MINA is sitting in an armchair doing embroidery. She looks up as there is a tap on the door and GERDA comes in.

> MINA:
> What is it Gerda?

> GERDA:
> It's about Mr. Arthur'm. Will he not be back tonight?

> MINA:
> No, he's gone to Ingstadt on business. He will be returning first thing in the morning.

> GERDA:
> Thank you Ma'am.

She is about to go when there is a knock on the outside door.

GERDA leaves without shutting the sitting room door, and we hear her open the front door, and a low murmer of voices for a moment.

Then she appears again in the sitting room door.

(68 - 69)

INT. SITTING ROOM. NIGHT (Cont'd)

> GERDA:
> There's a young lad Ma'am....he has a message for you....personal he said, wouldn't give it to me.

MINA gets to her feet.

> MINA:
> Alright Gerda.... I'll see him.

GERDA leaves as MINA crosses to the door and out.

70. <u>INT. HALL. NIGHT.</u>

GERDA'S broad back is just disappearing into the kitchen as MINA comes out and goes to the front door which stands open.

On the threshold is a young boy about fourteen, poorly dressed.

> LAD:
> You Mrs. Holmwood?

> MINA:
> I am.

> LAD:
> Got a message for you. You're to go to 49 Frederickstrasse.....right away he says, and you're not to tell anyone.

> MINA:
> Who says?

> LAD:
> Arthur Holmwood he call himself...said you'd know him.

> MINA:
> I know him of course.....but are you sure there's no mistake.....Mr. Holmwood has gone to Ingstadt.

> LAD:
> Not if he gives me this message he'asn't.....and he gives me this message.....night.

He touches his cap, turns and goes.

MINA shuts the door slowly behind her.

Then she makes up her mind, and starts over to the hall stand.

(69 - 70)

74.

INT. HALL. NIGHT. (Cont'd)

There she takes down a cloak and slips it on.

Then she comes back to the front door, opens it quietly, and slips out.

As the front door shuts behind her, GERDA appears in the door to the kitchen looking towards the front door.

           CUT TO:

71. INT. FRONTIER POST. NIGHT.

This is a blockhouse type of place and contains a large desk behind which sits a rather overblown customs official, or their 1890 equivalent. He has obviously been dragged out of his bed and wears a weird mixture of night attire and uniform.

ARTHUR is standing a little way back, while HESLING is standing across the desk from the OFFICIAL. Both HELSING and ARTHUR are travel stained.

    HESLING:
(with barely surpressed impatience) I will explain the whole thing to you again......just over four weeks ago a hearse was driven through here......in that....

    OFFICIAL:
(cutting in) Was you here?

    HESLING:
No I wasn't.

    OFFICIAL:
(with pride) The 'Ow do you know it came through here?

    HESLING:
It came from Klausenburgh and it went to Carlstadt.....how else would such a journey be accomplished, except by coming through here?

    OFFICIAL:
(reluctantly) True....true....anyhow, carry on.

    HESLING:
In that hearse was a coffin. We wish to know to where that coffin was consigned.

            (70 - 71)

INT. FRONTIER POST. NIGHT

> OFFICIAL:
> (pompously) Not at all sure I can tell you that you know.....(quickly) not that we don't keep official records, everything is done official here....we've got records back there of everything that's come through here in the last ten years.

> HESLING:
> Then I'll trouble you to get back there and find out what I want to know.

> OFFICIAL:
> That sort of attitude won't get us anywhere, will it. Like I said, I'm not sure I should let you know.

> HESLING:
> But you didn't say that. You said that you didn't know whether you were capable of giving us the information we seek. You have now established that you are in fact capable, but unwilling. There's a wealth of difference.

The OFFICIAL looks at HESLING for a moment trying to understand what on earth he's talking about. He falls back on his previous tack.

> OFFICIAL:
> That sort of attitude won't get us anywhere.

> HESLING:
> What sort of attitude?

Again the OFFICIAL is temporarily stumped. But he holds the trump card.

> OFFICIAL
> I'm not telling you anything.

HESLING moves closer to him, looking him in the eye.

> HESLING:
> Look my friend....either you give me the information I require or accept the consequences.

> OFFICIAL:
> What are the consequences?

Suddenly HESLING blazes.

> HESLING:
> I am the consequences....(shouts) Give me that information!

(71)

76.

INT. FRONTIER POST. NIGHT. (Cont'd)

The OFFICIAL all pomposity gone, gets from his stool and scuttles through a door behind his desk.

HESLING and ARTHUR exchange a glance - the OFFICIAL re-appears carrying a large overstuffed file.

He climbs back on his stool and starts to thumb through the file.

          OFFICIAL:
    Klausenburgh to Carlstadt you said....four weeks
    ago.....

He extracts a slip of paper from the file, and passes it across to HESLING.

          OFFICIAL:
    Here it is......sir.

HESLING looks at it and shows it to ARTHUR.

          HESLING:
    This is what we want. If we start back now
    we should get to Carlstadt by morning. As
    soon as the establishment opens we'll pay a
    call on this Mr......

He looks at the paper again.

    ......Mr. Marx.

                    CUT:

72.   EXT. UNDERTAKERS. NIGHT

We start on a notice saying.

        J.MARX   UNDERTAKER AND MORTICIAN

We PAN down from the sign to show the empty street.

After a moment MINA turns the corner and starts towards us. She is looking up at the street numbers.

Finally outside MARX she stops, approaches the door and knocks.

The knock reverberates inside the establishment, but there is no answering glimmer of light or sound.

She steps back and looks up at the sign again. Then she knocks once more.

Still there is no answer.

                          (71 - 72)

EXT. UNDERTAKER'S NIGHT. (Cont'd)

So she steps from the shadow of the door and looks along the road.

Adjoining the house is a yard, hidden by a high fence. Half way along the fence is another door, used for goods delivery. Over the door is another plaque marking the yard as belonging to MARX.

MINA starts along the road until she reaches the steps.

She hesitates for a moment, then walks down into -

73. EXT. UNDERTAKER'S YARD. NIGHT.

The eyeline that presents itself to MINA is that of a small yard bounded on three sides by the high walls of the neighbouring houses.

The yard itself is littered with half carved tombstones and effigies some of which appear in the halflight like monstrous ill formed creatures.

Against one of the walls is a section of the yard devoted to the manufacture of coffins, and a bunch of completed ones are stacked against one wall with their lids off.

Slowly MINA steps over the threshold of the gate and looks around her.

There is no-one there, no-one to meet her.

C.S. MINA

She looks around her nervously, then her glance fixes.

EYELINE

At one side of the yard there is a small door let into the high wall that surrounds it. The door is standing, slightly ajar, and through it can be seen the faintest thread of light.

M.S.

After a moments hesitation MINA starts across the yard towards the door, picking her way fearfully around the huge half carved effigies which grin and leer at her.

C.S. AT DOOR

MINA comes into frame and stands outside the door for a moment hesitating whether to go in. Then she makes up her mind and reaches out and pushes the door open.

(72 - 73)

EXT. UNDERTAKER'S YARD. NIGHT. (Cont'd)

                MINA:
(calling) Arthur......

She waits a moment and when there is no reply she steps inside.

74. INT. MORGUE STEPS. NIGHT.

She is at the top of a flight of stone steps which curve down out of sight. The light is looking up from somewhere downstairs.

She stands, listening. She hears a slight noise off - calls again

                MINA:
Arthur...

75. INT. MORGUE. NIGHT.

MINA comes round the bend in the stairs and looks about her.

The morgue is just that. It is a place for storing coffins which are occupied with cadavers, until they are taken away for burial.

The are placed haphazardly mostly, stacked on one another.
Some are ornate affairs with gleaming brasses, others are plain wooden boxes.

The light is supplied by an oil lamp set in a niche in the wall.

C.S. MINA

As she looks around her the fear is beginning to build up inside of her. Her glances start to wander wildly. Then it fixes out of shot.

C.S. LARGE COFFIN

This is the coffin we last saw on the hearse leaving the Dracula House. It now rests to two hestles. The lid has shifted very slightly, and even as we see it it slides back and a long bony hand appears over the edge.

C.S. MINA

This is a very big close up, and as she screams, clapping her hand to her mouth, we:

                            DISSOLVE:

(73 - 75)

76. INT. SITTING ROOM. DAY.

It is quite early in the morning, although it is daylight.

HESLING and ARTHUR are standing by a table in the window, still wearing their travelling cloaks. GERDA is pouring them some coffee.

> GERDA:
>
> .....stepping out all night then not even taking time for a proper breakfast.....whatever it is you're doing it'll wait till you've had a bite to eat........please sir, let me fry you some eggs?

> ARTHUR:
> We haven't time. Gerda? Is my wife up yet?

> GERDA:
>
> I haven't seen her, sir.....would you like me to call her?

> ARTHUR:
> Perhaps she has overslept....just look into her room quietly....if she is still sleeping, leave her.

GERDA goes out towards the hall. HESLING finishes his coffee wipes his mouth with his napkin. He looks at his watch.

> HESLING:
>
> Ready?

ARTHUR nods, downing the remainder of his coffee, and getting to his feet then he turns as GERDA comes hurrying back in.

> GERDA:
> She's not there sir....her bed's all made up and she's not there.

ARTHUR and HESLING exchange quick glances.

> ARTHUR:
> When did you last see.....?

> MINA:
> (off) Good morning.

They all turn in the direction of the voice.

C.S. MINA

She is standing in the door to the kitchen, looking radiant. She is dressed and is wearing a high necked collar.

(76)

INT. SITTING ROOM. DAY. (Cont'd)

She steps forward into the room.

                MINA:
    You gentlemen returned earlier than I expected
    .....thank you Gerda....

Gerda moves out to the kitchen.

    .... I awoke early and went for a long walk.....
    it was quite delightful.

ARTHUR steps forward and kisses her on the cheek.

                ARTHUR:
    We have to go out again now my dear....I am
    sorry to have to leave you alone like this.

                MINA:
    Don't worry about me, I'm perfectly alright.
    Indeed it was quite a luxury to have the house
    to myself last night.....

C.S. MINA

                MINA:
    (cont'd) I retired early and slept like a log.

                DISSOLVE:

77.   EXT. UNDERTAKER'S YARD. DAY.

From the back of the main building comes a small man, followed by
HESLING and ARTHUR. The small man is MARX.

He leads across the yard towards a small brick built outbuilding,
talking back over his shoulder all the while.

                MARX:
    I am delighted that you gentlemen finally
    arrived. It is common practise for us to
    pick up the remains of a dear one and transport
    him or her to the city here, but I'm bound to
    admit that the remains are always called for
    within two or three days of arrival........yes,
    indeed, I was getting quite worried about this
    particular case....it is nearly three weeks now
    you understand......

He stops outside the door to the small outbuilding and steps back
for the other two to proceed him.

                (76 - 77)

EXT. UNDERTAKER'S YARD. DAY (Cont'd)

          MARX:
          This is the entrance to our cellars.....
          We kept the corpses....the remains of the
          dear ones in the cool of the cellar.....you
          are gentleman of the world, there's no need
          for me to explain why, is there........
          after you.

HESLING and ARTHUR, both bending low, go through the door into the outbuilding.

78.   INT. MORGUE. DAY

We are shooting towards the steps that lead down into the morgue.

Around us are arranged the many coffins of varying degrees of opulence. Each one has a little tie on label attached to a convenient handle

We hear the voice of MARX.

          MARX:
          (Off) Perhaps you should let me lead the way......
          I know these stairs well.....they can be dangerous...
          we wouldn't want to have an accident would we.....

He appears round the slight bend in the stairs followed by HESLING and ARTHUR.

          MARX:
          (cont'd) An old man called here once to see his
          dear departed.....he fell down those stairs....
          really it was quite amusing.... he called to pay
          his last respects, and he remained to share them...
          quite amusing.

They reach floor level, and MARX stands for a moment looking around him.

          MARX:
          Now where are we....somewhere at the back. I
          shouldn't wonder....the thing has been here so
          long it's bound to be at the back isn't it....
          now, where was it....where was it.

He accidentally kicks one of the coffins rather hard.

          MARX:
          Oops, sorry.....

(77 - 78)

INT. MORGUE. DAY. (Cont'd)

He turns to the watching ARTHUR and HESLING.

>MARX:
>You'll have to excuse me....I always speak to them this way.....one becomes...how shall I say it....friendly with them after a while.... this one here for example....

He points to the one he kicked.

>....charming girl...really charming.

He smiles a trifle simply at them and continues into the back of the morgue.

C.S. ARTHUR AND HESLING

The look at one another.

Then they are pulled round by a voice from MARX.

>MARX:
>(Off) Now there's an extraordinary thing.....

They exchange glances again, then, with HESLING leading they hurry over to join MARX.

He is staring at something out of shot.

>MARX:
>It was there, I know it was....I saw it only yesterday.....

HESLING and ARTHUR look to where he is looking.

C.S. FLOOR OF MORGUE

The trestles are still there, but of the coffin there is no sign.

>MARX:
>(over) I really cannot understand who could have moved it....this is quite beyond me.

>DISSOLVE:

79. INT. SITTING ROOM. NIGHT.

ARTHUR is seated, HESLING is pacing up and down in front of him.

MINA is sitting across from ARTHUR doing embroidery.

(78 - 79)

INT. SITTING ROOM. NIGHT. (Cont'd)

          HESLING:
The only thing we can hope for now is that he has returned to his home....

          ARTHUR:
Then that is where we must go.

          HESLING:
(shakes head) Once he has gone to earth there we'll never find him. Be assured that he won't just hide in his mausoleum....the place is honeycombed with underground passages.

          ARTHUR:
We'll tear the place down....stone by stone.

HESLING gives him a warning glance.

GERDA comes in from the kitchen.

          GERDA:
Will you all be in to dinner tonight ma'am ?

          ARTHUR:
You'll stay Hesling ?

          HESLING:
Thank you.

          GERDA:
How about you ma'am ?

          MINA:
Of course...you know I will.

          GERDA:
Sorry ma'am....but what with you going out last night just when I get everything cooked... I just wanted to be sure.

She leaves, as MINA flashes a quick glance at the two men. But neither seem to be taking any notice. MINA lowers her eyes and continues with her embroidery.

After a beat, HESLING looks up thoughtfully at MINA

          DISSOLVE:

80.   <u>INT. SITTING ROOM. NIGHT.</u>

Dinner is nearly over. The table has been set up in the sitting room, and now coffee and liqueurs are in evidence. Both of the men are smoking.

HESLING has just said something that has MINA laugh nervously.

(79 - 80)

INT. SITTING ROOM. NIGHT (Cont'd)

          MINA:
You're just trying to frighten me Doctor
Hesling with those ghost stories of yours.

          HESLING:
But it's true, I swear it. I tell you there
is no accounting the things that some of these
country people will say.

          MINA:
You can't expect me to believe that anyone
could be so simple.

          HESLING:
Just as I have described it to you....and more
even....

          MINA:
Oh no.....more I cannot believe.

          HESLING:
It's true. Do you know that there is a district
in Transylvania that is supposed to be cursed....
by the devil. In this hamlet, it is hardly more
than that, the occupants are convinced that they
and their descendents are forever under the devil's
command. No amount of talk or persuasion by
visiting clerics will convince them otherwise. If
cursed by the devil they are supposed to be, then
that is their lot, and they are satisfied with it.
They won't even allow any Holy symbols in the hamlet.
I went there once, and they searched me...they took
this from me.....

He takes his crucifix from his pocket, the one he used to burn LUCY.

          ....and they would not return it until I left
          them.

The production of the crucifix seems to have had a peculiar effect
on MINA. Though outwardly the same, she seems to have shrunk a
little inside herself, and where there was merriment in her eyes,
there is now something else, something that could be fear.

HESLING hold the crucifix up, so that it catches the light.

          HESLING:
Simply a piece of metal wrought in a certain
fashion. Had the same piece of metal been
wrought any other way, it's significance would
be lost.....it is what it represents that they
feared, not what it is....here Miss Mina, catch....

(80)

INT. SITTING ROOM. NIGHT. (Cont'd)

Suddenly he pitches the crucifix across the table towards her.

In voluntarily, MINA reaches out to catch it, then she draws her hand away quickly, as though realising what she is doing. But not quickly enough.

The crucifix strikes her on the back of her hand.

She utters a sharp cry of pain, and puts her other hand over the back of the hand where the crucifix touched.

ARTHUR meanwhile has jumped to his feet.

He and HESLING are looking towards MINA.

Slowly she takes her covering hand off the affected part.

C.S. MINA'S HAND.

Burned into the flesh is the mark of the cross where it landed on her. It is a similar burn to the one that LUCY received on the forehead in the same circumstances.

C.S. MINA

Looking down at her hand. Slowly she brings it up into frame. Then she turns and looks at the two men.

C.S. HESLING AND ARTHUR

They are staring towards her.

C.S. MINA

Suddenly she bursts into tears, gets up and runs from the room.

C.S. ARTHUR AND HESLING

>	HESLING:
>	(to himself) Fool I've been....what a fool.

ARTHUR suddenly leaps to his feet to follow MINA. HESLING grabs his arm.

>	HESLING:
>	You can do nothing.

ARTHUR looks at him wildly.

>	HESLING:
>	(quietly but firmly) There's nothing you
>	can do now.

INT. SITTING ROOM. NIGHT. (Cont'd)

HESLING forces the dazed ARTHUR to sit down.

          ARTHUR:
(aghast) How can this have happened?

          HESLING:
He failed with Lucy, now he's trying to get Mina.

          ARTHUR:
(bitterly) Trying...he's succeeded.

          HESLING:
Not yet, Holmwood. You and I must stop him. We must stand guard all night....he must not be able to get near the house.

          ARTHUR:
How do we stop him?

HESLING moves over and picks up the crucifix from where it fell.

          HESLING:
....This is sufficient to keep him at bay. He cannot pass beyond it.

ARTHUR looks up from where he is sitting.

          ARTHUR:
And Mina, is there any hope?

          HESLING:
Hope? Of course there is hope. Until she dies she cannot become one of the Damned. We must see that she does not die. Now you will take the front of the house, I the rear. It will be a long and lonely vigil....but if it serves it's purpose it will be worth it a thousand times over.

                            DISSOLVE:

(80)

87.

81. EXT. HOLMWOOD GARDEN. LOT OR STUDIO. NIGHT.

   HESLING is on guard, alert, watchful. His eyes search the bushes around him.

82. EXT BACK OF HOLMWOOD HOUSE. LOT. NIGHT.

   ARTHUR, too, stands on guard. Not surprisingly, he looks very apprehensive. He glances at his pocket watch, then back towards the house.

83. EXT. BEDROOM WINDOW. NIGHT.

   Behind the half-drawn curtains a light shines.

84. EXT. BACK OF HOLMWOOD HOUSE. NIGHT.

   ARTHUR breathes a sigh of relief, carries on his vigil.

85. INT. MINA'S & ARTHUR'S ROOM. STUDIO. NIGHT.

   MINA is standing by the window, hidden from view by the half-drawn curtain, watching.

   She turns away, and we see that her eyes are blazing.

   She crosses to the door and stands listening. After a moment, she seems to hear something for she unlocks the door and opens it.

86. INT. HALL. NIGHT.

   MINA comes into big foreground as she opens the door to her room. She stands there, quite still and expressionless, staring down into the hall below.

   The camera pans slowly from MINA across and down.

   Standing at the bottom of the stairs is DRACULA.

   He walks slowly towards us, starts to mount the stairs.

   C.S. MINA.

   She watches for a moment, then moves silently back into her room, leaving the door open.

   After a moment, DRACULA comes into shot and follows her into the bedroom. The door closes. Hold.

   (81 - 86)

87. INT. MINA & ARTHUR'S BEDROOM. NIGHT.

C.S. MINA

She stares at something past camera. Her eyes blaze, her lips are parted, she gasps for breath.

A shadow crosses her, and she closes her eyes. Her body begins to shake as if with fever.

B.C.S. DRACULA.

We see only his eyes, staring, staring....

TIGHT TWO-SHOT

DRACULA takes MINA into his arms. She moans quietly. He gently brushes her forehead with his full lips ... then her check... then her neck. MINA stops shuddering, holds her breath. Then -

SHOCK CUT TO:

88. EXT. TREE. NIGHT.

C.S. OWL

The owl hoots and flies off with flapping wings.

89. EXT. BACK OF HOLMWOOD HOUSE. NIGHT.

ARTHUR starts, looks up at the tree, follows the flying of the owl.

He takes a deep breath, glances once more at the still lighted window, mops his brow, then continues his vigil.

FADE OUT:

FADE IN:

90. EXT. BACK OF HOLMWOOD HOUSE. DAWN.

Fingers of light are streaking the sky.

ARTHUR is standing just inside the porch. He is cold, tired and hungry.

(87-90)

90. EXT. BACK OF HOLMWOOD HOUSE. DAWN. (Cont'd)

But nevertheless he springs to wakefullness as there is the sound of a footstep crunching in the gravel.

It is HESLING.

He comes up to where ARTHUR is standing.

>HESLING:
>It is nearly light ....he will not come now.

He sees ARTHUR looking very low.

>... cheer up my friend, we have succeeded in what we set out to do...we have kept him away from your MINA all night. Come, let us go in.

They enter.

91. INT. HALL. DAWN.

The two men come in and start to remove their cloaks. ARTHUR, still looking woebegone, heads for the door of MINA's room.

HESLING watches him to the door, then turns and starts towards the kitchen.

He spins round at a cry from ARTHUR.

>ARTHUR:
>Mina....!

ARTHUR is standing in the door to the bedroom, looking in.

HESLING rushes to him and looks into the room too.

92. INT. MINA'S & ARTHUR'S ROOM. DAWN.

Stretched across the bed, out of the bedclothes is the figure of MINA.

There is blood everywhere.

It stains the whiteness of the bed linen, it is smeared across the front of MINA'S nightdress, it is splodged across the large expanse of bare chest that protrudes from the neck of the nightdress, and it is spread across her face.

(90 - 92)

92. INT. MINA'S & ARTHUR'S ROOM. DAWN (Cont'd)

In her neck are the two marks, from which there still runs a trickle of blood adding to that already present.

DISSOLVE:

93. INT. MINA'S & ARTHUR'S BEDROOM. DUSK.

It is much later the same day.

MINA now lays beneath the bedclothes and everything has been tidied up.

In an armchair next to MINA'S bed, sits ARTHUR. He has no jacket on and his sleeves are rolled up.

Connected to one arm, under a roll of bandage is a tube which runs to MINA'S arm, also under a roll of bandage.

ARTHUR is staring at the ceiling, MINA still has her eyes closed and looks like death, and HESLING is listening to MINA with an 1899 stethescope.

GERDA stands there, watching fascinated.

HESLING straightens up, and moves round to look down at ARTHUR.

He takes ARTHUR'S wrist and feels his pulse.

Then he releases ARTHUR'S arm, and starts to undo the bandages from around the arm.

> ARTHUR:
> Has she had enough?

> HESLING:
> For the moment. Anyway, you have given enough...you cannot spare any more.

ARTHUR sits up and swings his feet to the floor. He starts to roll down his sleeve, then a wave of giddiness overtakes him and he puts his hand to his head.

> HESLING:
> Are you alright?

(92 - 93)

93.   INT. MINA'S & ARTHUR'S BEDROOM. DAY. (Cont'd)

ARTHUR nods.

> ARTHUR:
> Just a little dizzy.

> HESLING:
> That will wear off.

ARTHUR gets up and goes across to the bed and looks down at MINA.

C.S. MINA

Eyes closed, motionless, white as death. But we can see that she is still breathing.

C.S. ARTHUR

Looking down at her. After a moment HESLING comes in making it a two shot.

> ARTHUR:
> Will she be alright?

> HESLING:
> If she is allowed to rest peacefully.
> (turning to Arthur) And you must rest, too.

Apparently he has not heard.

> ARTHUR:
> How did he get in here? We were watching all night.

> HESLING:
> (firmly) Go and lie down - I'll join you later.

He ushers ARTHUR to the door.

> HESLING:
> (intercepting any protest) Gerda and I will watch over your Mina.

He closes the door on ARTHUR and moves back to the bed.

GERDA watches him fascinated. HESLING remembers she is there, gives her a tired smile.

(93)

93. INT MINA'S & ARTHUR'S BEDROOM DAY. DAY. (Cont'd)

                      HESLING:
Would you be so kind as to bathe
Mrs. Holmwood's forehead, Gerda?

Gerda jumps to obey, glad at last to be able to help.

HESLING starts to clear up.

                                    MIX TO:

No page 93 per original

95. INT SITTING ROOM. NIGHT.

ARTHUR is seated, sipping a glass of red wine. He jumps up as HESLING enters.

          ARTHUR:
There's only one solution - your theories are wrong. He can change himself into....something else....he must be able to.

HESLING will have none of this.

          HESLING:
No, no.

          ARTHUR:
Then how else could he have got in ? We were there all night.

          HESLING:
He could have slipped past us.... we're not infallable....surely that's it...... and yet.....?

GERDA comes in. HESLING turns on her.

          HESLING:
I thought I told you to look after Mrs. Holmwood.

          GERDA:
She's all right, sir. she's sleeping. I was wondering whether you might want some of mine sir.

HESLING stares at her.

          GERDA:
(explaining) My blood, sir. For poor Mrs. Holmwood.

          HESLING:
Thank you, Gerda, but I don't think that it will be necessary.

GERDA breathes a sigh of relief, she had not relished the idea really.

          GERDA:
Well, I won't pretend I'm not glad sir.

She starts to leave then hesitates.

          GERDA:
(to ARTHUR) I'm sorry to bother you, sir, but have you any idea what Mrs. Holmwood wanted me to do with that box in the cellar?

(95)

INT. LIVING ROOM. NIGHT. (Cont'd)

> ARTHUR:
> (Hardly hearing) What box, Gerda?
>
> GERDA:
> That long one, sir..

But before she can complete her sentence, HESLING has rushed past her and shot out of the door, leaving both GERDA and ARTHUR staring after him.

96. INT. CELLAR. NIGHT.

The cellar is dirty lit by moonlight from a dirty window.

We are shooting towards the steps. We see the door and HESLING rush down towards us.

He reaches the bottom of the stairs, and looks around him. Then his glance freezes.

Laying to one side of the cellar, away from the wall, is a large wooden crate.

M.S.

Still holding the lamp aloft, HESLING moves over towards the crate.

He pauses by it for a moment, then he throws back the lid and looks inside.

C.S. INT. CRATE

In the crate is the coffin of Dracula.

The polished wood gleams dully, while the brass fitments give off scintillating reflections from HELSING'S light.

Carved into a plate on the lid of the coffin is the single word.

> DRACULA

C.S. HESLING

Bending down, he lifts the lid of the coffin, throwing it back.

C.S. INTO COFFIN

In the coffin is a layer of soil at the bottom. Pressed into the soil is the clear indentation where Dracula has lain.

But no Dracula.

(95 - 96)

INT. CELLAR. NIGHT. (Cont'd)

C.S. HESLING

Looking down into the coffin.

C.S. DRACULA

He is standing at the top of the cellar steps. He looks malevolently at HESLING for an instant, then he turns and goes out.

C.S. HESLING

The sound of the cellar door slamming from the top of the stairs pulls him round.

He starts towards the stairs, then stops. Reaching in his pocket he pulls out the crucifix. He turns back and throws it into the coffin.

C.S. INTO COFFIN

The crucifix catches the reflected light and gleams into CAMERA.

M.S.

HESLING has run up the stairs to the door at the top.

He tries to open it but it is locked.

He bangs hard on the door with his fist.

> HESLING:
> Open the door.....Holmwood....can you hear me ?

He bangs again, then steps as there is the sound of hurried foot steps outside.

Then the door opens to disclose ARTHUR

HESLING pushes past him.

97. INT. HALL. NIGHT.

HESLING pushes into the hall and looks around him quickly.

> ARTHUR:
> What is it.....was it there?

> HESLING:
> It was there....empty.

> ARTHUR:
> Then where is....?

(96 - 97)

INT. HALL. NIGHT. (Cont'd)

Suddenly there is a piercing scream from the direction of MINA'S room.

Both men turn and run towards the room pushing the door open.

98. INT MINA'S ROOM. NIGHT.

GERDA is crouched in one corner of the room, staring fearfully towards the French Windows which are open, the curtains billowing in the wind.

Of MINA there is no sign.

GERDA sees the two men and starts to get to her feet. She is in a terrible state.

ARTHUR runs straight for the French Windows and out, HELSING goes to GERDA.

>GERDA:
>....he crashes open the door....his eyes were glowing something dreadful....he picked poor Mrs. Holmwood up like she were a baby....his cloak flapped about him as he ran out like a giant bat. It was terrible sir....poor Mrs. Holmwood... what's happened to her.....who was he...what's he done to Mrs. Holmwood..

>HESLING:
>(over GERDA'S speech) There there Gerda..... calm yourself....we'll get Mrs. Holmwood back..

He turns as ARTHUR comes back in through the French Windows.

>ARTHUR:
>(over GERDA'S speech) No sign....he crossed the garden and went over the wall at the end, I can see the tracks.

>HESLING:
>(over GERDA'S speech) We must follow him. He can only make for one place now, his home, he's got to get to his native soil before the sun rises....it's his only chance.

>ARTHUR:
>Mina ?

>HESLING:
>If we can catch up with him before he reaches his own sanctuary, we'll save her. He has a long way to go before the sun up...the first thing he'll have to do is to find himself a coach.
>   CUT TO:

99. **EXT. MAIN ROAD. NIGHT.**

This is a road on the outskirts of Town.

There is a coach and pair rattling along the road.

C.S. DRIVER

He is whistling quietly to himself, enjoying the night air.

Now he concentrates on something ahead of him, and starts to rein the horses.

EYELINE

Laying in the road is the figure of a woman (MINA) dressed in white.

M.S.

The coach comes to a stop with the horses barely three feet away from MINA.

The horses paw the ground, their breath condensing in clouds of steam, as they toss their heads nervously.

The driver knots the reins quickly and jumps down from his seat and makes his way to the head of the horses and the figure in the road.

          DRIVER:
    'Ullo, what's this?

MINA is laying on her side, she is still unconscious.

The DRIVER goes down on one knee and starts to try and lift her.

          DRIVER:
    My gaud what's 'appened to her ?

Then a noise off catches his attention. He turns.

C.S. DRACULA

This is a low angle from the drivers viewpoint. DRACULA looks high above him, his cloak flapping about him.

His eyes blaze with anger.

As DRACULA moves downwards we:

                        DISSOLVE:

100. EXT. MAIN ROAD. NIGHT.

About half an hour later.

Where there was a coach and pair, there is now HESLING'S small open coach, which he drives himself.

In foreground, bending over a still figure are ARTHUR and HESLING.

The figure if we see him is that of the DRIVER.

>HESLING:
>Throat cut.....

He puts his fingers to the blood on the man's neck, and then runs his fingers together.

>HESLING:
>.....about half an hour ago. Come on.

The two of them race back to the coach and clamber on.

HESLING unknots the reins, whips up the horses and the coach leaps off.

101. INT. COACH. NIGHT.

ARTHUR is hanging on tight as HESLING urges the horses to a cracking pace. They have to shout above the clatter of the hooves and the roar of steel-tired wheels.

>HESLING:
>(shouts) So he's got his coach, and he's half an hour ahead of us.....we must catch up with him.

>ARTHUR:
>(shouts) What will he do when he gets to his home ?

>HESLING:
>He'll bury himself...somewhere where we won't be able to find him. He can stay buried as long as he wants to....years if necessary.

>ARTHUR:
>And Mina ?

HESLING looks at ARTHUR a trifle sheepishly, and says nothing.

>ARTHUR:
>Did you hear me.....I said what about Mina?

HESLING glances at ARTHUR then he makes up his mind, looks ahead again.

(100 - 101)

INT. COACH. NIGHT (Cont'd)

> HESLING:
> There is one way he can make sure that Mina stays with him...he can bury her too. If she dies while enclosed in Dracula's native soil, she will rise again when he chooses to call.

> ARTHUR:
> You mean he might....bury her alive?

HESLING nods as we:

DISSOLVE:

102. EXT. FRONTIER POST. LOT. NIGHT

All is quiet and deserted.

In the distance, a rumble of coach wheels builds to a roar as DRACULA'S coach approaches at full gallop. DRACULA is lashing the foaming horses in a frenzy.

He races through the wooden barrier without slowing down.

103. INT. FRONTIER POST. STUDIO. NIGHT.

The OFFICIAL comes out from his room at the back. He has obviously been asleep as he still wears his long nightshirt. He mutters to himself as he buckles on his revolver.

Suddenly there is an almighty crash. The OFFICIAL nearly drops dead with shock, then runs to the door.

104. EXT. FRONTIER POST. NIGHT

DRACULA'S coach has just crashed through the barrier.

The OFFICIAL rushes out and stands rooted. He just cannot believe the evidence of his eyes.

SOFT WIPE TO:

105. EXT. INN LOT. NIGHT.

DRACULA'S coach shatters the night silence of the sleeping village as it crashes through the cobbled street.

As it disappears around a bend a light appears in the window of the Inn.

CUT TO:

(101 - 105)

106. **EXT. FRONTIER POST. NIGHT.**

C.S. OFFICIAL.

Now wearing an overcoat and boots over his nightshirt, his cap on his head, he is just completing a temporary repair on the barrier.

Suddenly he stops his muttered profanities and listens.

In the distance we hear the rumble of a second coach.

The OFFICIAL spins round as we see HESLING'S coach approaching. He rushes out into the road, his arms waving wildly.

The coach shudders to a screeching halt.

C.S. COACH

> HESLING:
> (shouts) A coach and pair came through here....
> how long ago?

C.S. OFFICIAL

> OFFICIAL:
> It's you is it!

> HESLING:
> How long ago ?

M.S.

> OFFICIAL:
> About half an hour.

> HESLING:
> Then open up the barrier.

> OFFICIAL:
> (smugly) Can't do that, there's the formalities.

He turns to the door of his Post.

> OFFICIAL:
> Now if you gentlemen will follow me...

Once more he is stopped by the sound of a coach crashing through the barrier.

He turns slowly and rushes off at what we know is a pile of splintered wood.

> SOFT WIPE TO:

107. EXT. INN. NIGHT.

There are now lights in the windows of the Inn and the LANDLORD and a couple of GUESTS are in the street, disturbed by the night ride of the vampire.

A second coach is hear approaching. The MEN press themselves back against the wall as HESLING'S coach sways through and away.

The MEN shake their heads. Nothing like this has happened in the village since the last wolf hunt.

108. EXT. COUNTRY ROAD. PRE - DAWN.

This is the same road we saw in the first sequence, the road that leads to the House of Dracula.

HESLING'S coach comes rattling along; HESLING is driving the horses hard.

109. INT. COACH. PRE - DAWN

ARTHUR indicates something o/s.

110. EXT. HOUSE OF DRACULA. LOT. PRE - DAWN

Eyeline - unsteady.

The House can be seen through the trees, the turrets and castellates walls rising from the trees that surround it.

111. INT. COACH. PRE - DAWN

> ARTHUR:
> (shouts) It's getting light...what are you going to do?
>
> HESLING:
> (shouts) We must see what has already been done.

112. EXT. HOUSE OF DRACULA. PRE - DAWN.

This is in the grounds, a few yards from the mausoleum.

A small grave has been dug. Even as we see it we see DRACULA pick up the figure of MINA and throw her into the grave as if she were a doll. Then he starts to shovel in the earth on top of her.

C.S. INTO GRAVE

MINA chooses this moment to regain conciousness. She opens her eyes just as a shovelful of earth lands on her chest.

For a moment she is unable to orientate herself, then she sees what is happening and starts to scream.

(107 - 112)

EXT. HOUSE OF DRACULA.   PRE - DAWN   (Cont'd)

C.S. DRACULA

This is from MINA's eyeline inside the grave. We see DRACULA lift another spadeful of earth, then tip it down at CAMERA. The earth lands across the lens, blotting out the picture.

C.S. DRACULA

He shovels another spadeful in, then he stops as he hears the sound of a coach.

113.   EXT. HOUSE OF DRACULA PRE - DAWN

HESLING'S coach rattles to a stop and the two men pile out.

Standing in the drive is the coach and pair that DRACULA used.

The horses are standing with lowered heads in the harness, their bodies lathered with sweat.

HESLING and ARTHUR jump down, HESLING looking off towards the mausoleum.

Then he points out.

L.S. DRACULA

He shovels one more spadeful into the grave, then he drops the shovel and starts towards the house.

C.S. ARTHUR and HESLING

ARTHUR hurries off towards the grave, cutting through the under-brush, while HESLING starts running up the drive.

133A.   M.S.

He reaches the front door a couple of seconds after DRACULA.

He runs straight in.

134.   INT. DRACULA HALL. PRE - DAWN.

HESLING stops for a moment inside the door trying to tell which way DRACULA has run.

Then he hears a noise coming from the direction of the Dining Room.

He runs towards the open door.

115.   INT. DRACULA DINING ROOM. PRE - DAWN.

As HESLING comes in, he looks up and sees DRACULA running along the gallery

(112 - 115)

INT. DRACULA DINING ROOM. PRE - DAWN (Cont'd)

He flies up the stairs after him.

116. INT PASSAGE. PRE - DAWN

HESLING appears and looks up and down. Of DRACULA there is no sign.

The he hears a noise from a door at the end of the passage, the door that leads to the Gothic room.

He races up the passage and throws open the door.

117. INT. GOTHIC ROOM. DAWN

This is the room where Jonathon had the encounter with the woman in sequence one.

The light through the stained glass windows is just beginning to pick out the colours of the window on the dust covered floor.

In the centre of a raised dais DRACULA is lifting a heavy stone trap in the floor.

C.S. HESLING

He sees what is happening. Quickly he closes the door behind him and locks it with a large key that is in the lock. He runs towards DRACULA taking a crucifix from his pocket.

M.S.

DRACULA is just heaving the trap fully open when HESLING reaches him and holding the crucifix in front of him he forces a snarling DRACULA to let go of the trap which slams shut again.

Then HESLING plants himself over the trap, looking at DRACULA.

C.S. HESLING

Staring steadily at DRACULA

C.S. DRACULA

He is looking at HESLING, his blood red eyes flooded with anger, unable to do anything for a moment.

Then even while he is standing there a ray of sunlight creeps across his face.

He claps his hand to his face and screams, then he turns.

M.S.

HESLING uses the crucifix to force DRACULA back into the pool of light. (115 - 117)

105.

INT. GOTHIC ROOM. DAWN (Cont'd)

C.S. WINDOW

The sun is now beaming through the whole window, the colours sparkling and then beaming in the dust laden room.

C.S. DRACULA

He stands where he is for a moment not knowing what to do. Then he runs for the door that HESLING has locked. In so doing, he passes right through the light.

Before he can reach the door he falls headlong.

As he starts to try and scramble to his feet, we hear an ominous splintering, cracking sound.

C.S. DRACULA'S LEGS.

The trousered legs, scrabbling for a foothold seem suddenly to no longer contain let at all.

The solidity inside the trouser seems to Dissolve, and as the boots fall from the end of the trouser leg, a little pile of whitish powder cascades from both the boot and the trouser leg.

C.S. DRACULA

His face has started to powder too, the flesh drying fast and falling from the skull in the form of dust.

C.S. DRACULA's HANDS

The hands which are scrambling along the floor trying to reach the door. Suddenly the fingers start to break off, snapping at the joints, and they too start to dissolve into powder and dust.

C.S. DRACULA

The last sight of his face before it is no more. Before it dries up completely, and spreads itself in powder form across the floor.

118. EXT. HOUSE OF DRACULA. DAY

ARTHUR is bent over MINA who he has laid out on the grass.

She is laying there in an almost hypnotic condition. Then it is suddenly as though her mind clears. She looks towards ARTHUR who is bending over her and raises her hand to touch his arm.

ARTHUR starts to take her hand in his, when he exclaims surprise.

(117 - 118)

EXT. HOUSE OF DRACULA. DAY. (Cont'd)

They both look at MINA's hand.

INSERT

The mark of the cross very gradually fades away leaving the flesh clean.

TWO SHOT

They look at one another.

             MINA:
    He is dead.

ARTHUR starts to help her to her feet and we hear for the first time in this location the sound of birds singing.

The two of them make their way towards the drive, as from the house steps HESLING.

He pauses for a moment, sees the two of them and starts towards them as we:

                        FADE OUT:

    T H E   E N D

Dracula's distruction by Van Helsing - Cut from various version, from many countries, for being too gruesome

SHOWMAN'S MANUAL

ADVERTISING · PUBLICITY · EXPLOITATION

billing

Hammer Film Productions, Ltd.
Presents
"HORROR OF DRACULA"
Technicolor ®
starring
PETER CUSHING
also starring
MICHAEL GOUGH
and
MELISSA STRIBLING
with
CHRISTOPHER LEE
as DRACULA
Screenplay by
JIMMY SANGSTER
From the novel by
BRAM STOKER
Directed by
TERENCE FISHER
Executive Producer:
MICHAEL CARRERAS
Associate Producer:
ANTHONY NELSON-KEYS
Produced by
ANTHONY HINDS
A Universal-International Release

the staff

Production Manager, Don Weeks; Assistant Director, Robert Lynn; Continuity, Doreen Dearnaley; Director of Photography, Jack Asher, B.S.C.; Camera Operator, Len Harris; Sound Mixer, Jock May; Art Director, Bernard Robinson; Stills Cameraman, Tom Edwards; Supervising Editor, James Needs; Editor, Bill Lenny; Make Up Artist, Phil Leakey; Hairdresser, Henry Montsash; Wardrobe, Molly Arbuthnot; Musical Director, John Hollingsworth; Composer, James Bernard.

the cast

Van Helsing.......PETER CUSHING
Arthur Holmwood..........MICHAEL GOUGH
Mina Holmwood..........MELISSA STRIBLING
Count Dracula..........CHRISTOPHER LEE
Lucy..........CAROL MARSH
Jonathan Harker..........JOHN VAN EYSSEN
Marx, the Undertaker..........MILES MALLESON
Vampire Woman..........VALERIE GAUNT

the story

(Not for Publication)

A diary incriminating Count Dracula (CHRISTOPHER LEE) is found by Van Helsing (PETER CUSHING) in investigating the mysterious death of his friend, Jonathan Harker (JOHN VAN EYSSEN), apparently the victim of a blood-sucking vampire.

Van Helsing finds that Harker's fiancee, Lucy (CAROL MARSH), also has been attacked by a vampire. Lucy's brother, Arthur Holmwood (MICHAEL GOUGH), and his wife, Mina (MELISSA STRIBLING), join Van Helsing in attempting to track down the human monster.

Lucy succumbs, but Van Helsing is able to bring her back from the dead, and free her from Dracula's evil spell, by driving a wooden stake through her heart. Seemingly from out of nowhere Dracula strikes again, this time attacking Mina and carrying her off with him. He heads for his castle across the border.

Van Helsing and Arthur catch up with Dracula just as he is preparing a grave for Mina. Dracula seeks safety in the catacombs of the castle but Van Helsing forces him into a shaft of dawning sunlight — the only way in which Dracula can be killed.

Trapped in the beams of light, Dracula collapses and disintegrates. And with his passing Mina comes back to the world of mortal men, freed for all time from the satanic power of the blood-lusting vampire.

'Horror of Dracula' Stars Human Vampire

(Advance)

One of the world's classic monsters, the unforgettable human vampire of Bram Stoker's famous novel, comes to the screen in a completely new Color film when Hammer Film Productions, Ltd. presents "Horror of Dracula," opening .... at the .... Theatre.

The picture stars Peter Cushing, Michael Gough and Melissa Stribling with Christopher Lee as Dracula. "Horror of Dracula," which reunites Cushing and Lee after their successful shocker "The Curse of Frankenstein," is released by Universal-International.

All-New 'Horror of Dracula' Rates Tops Among All-Time Monster-Movie Masterpieces

(Review)

For devotees of the macabre, "Horror of Dracula" rates as a "must see."

A tale of vampires lusting for human blood, the completely new shock drama is now playing at the .... Theatre.

Few fictional characters are more horrendous than the evil Count Dracula, the "undead" fiend who has lived for untold centuries, feasting on the life blood of his victims.

Dracula is portrayed in all his frightful menace by Christopher Lee, remembered for his brilliant work in an earlier shocker, "The Curse of Frankenstein."

Few spectators will be able to withhold their screams when Dracula prepares to sink his lethal fangs into the soft flesh of one of the many lovely women numbered among his prey.

Dracula's nemesis is Van Helsing, the eminent Dutch physician played by Peter Cushing, and the women in the cast include three of England's most glamorous actresses, Melissa Stribling, Carol Marsh and Valerie Gaunt.

Audiences will have to take to their smelling salts or other restoratives at the "liberation" rites —the driving of a wooden stake through the heart of Dracula's victims — to free their soul from his power.

A product of Hammer Film Productions for Universal-International release, the Technicolor film was directed by Terence Fisher for producer Anthony Hinds.

Screenplay credit goes to Jimmy Sangster, who based the tale on the novel by Bram *Stoker*.

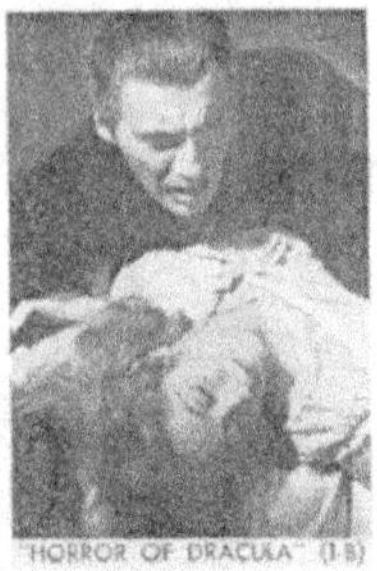

"HORROR OF DRACULA" (1-B)

FIENDISH Dracula, the human vampire, feasts on the blood of his victim, Melissa Stribling, in one of the terrifying moments in "Horror of Dracula," the new Hammer Film Productions, Ltd. Technicolor film based on the Bram Stoker classic. The Universal-International release stars Peter Cushing, Michael Gough and Miss Stribling with Christopher Lee as *Dracula*. *(Still 6820-22)*

Vampire Converts Three Beauties In Horror Film

(Current)

Three of England's loveliest actresses are suddenly transformed from respectable women into female vampires thirsting for human blood in "Horror of Dracula," the new Hammer Film Productions, Ltd. Technicolor motion picture based on Bram Stoker's horror classic, now playing at the .... Theatre.

The three beautiful actresses in this Universal-International release are Melissa Stribling, Carol Marsh and Valerie Gaunt, each of them in turn becoming victims then disciples of Count Dracula, literature's most famous of all master vampires. Miss Stribling is starred with Peter Cushing and Michael Gough with Christopher Lee as Dracula.

All three women were chosen for their petite, frail, innocent good looks. But when make-up man Phil Leakey did his frightful work the hapless trio had become drooling, long-fanged monsters. But this was no picnic for the girls. Miss Marsh had to lie in a coffin, scream for her supper and have a wooden stake driven through her evil heart. Ironically her previous acting part had been as Alice in "Alice in Wonderland."

Miss Stribling found herself buried deep in a grave with heavy Berkshire Clay shoveled over her and also got the stake treatment. Valerie Gaunt, an early victim of Dracula was first of the female vampire contingent in the picture.

"Horror of Dracula" was produced by the creators of "The Curse of Frankenstein."

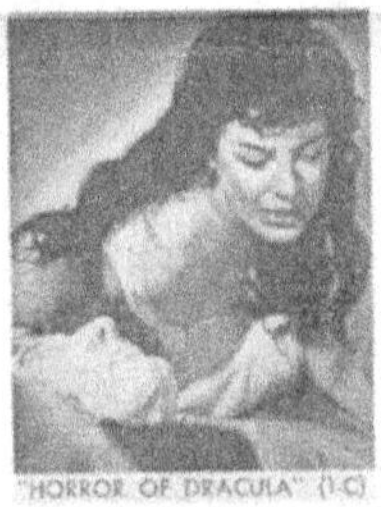

"HORROR OF DRACULA" (1-C)

VALERIE GAUNT plays the female vampire in "Horror of Dracula," the new Hammer Film Productions, Ltd. Technicolor film based on the Bram Stoker classic. The Universal-International release stars Peter Cushing, Michael Gough and Melissa Stribling, with Christopher Lee as Dracula. *(Still 6820-8AD)*

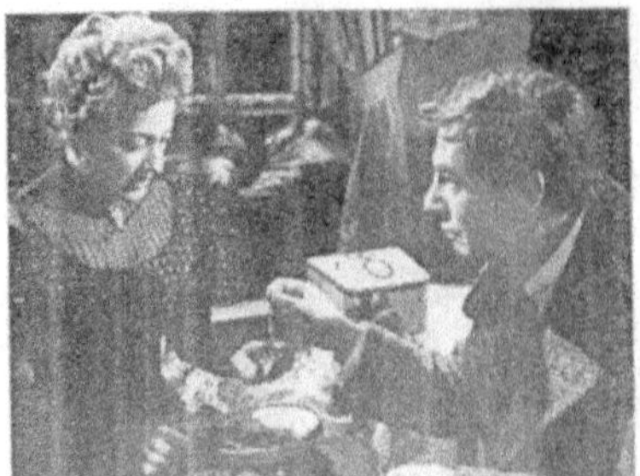

"HORROR OF DRACULA" (2-B)

MICHAEL GOUGH gives a crucifix to his wife, played by Melissa Stribling, to ward off the evil power of the human vampire, Dracula. This is a scene from "Horror of Dracula," the new Hammer Film Productions, Ltd. Technicolor film based on the Bram Stoker classic. The Universal-International release stars Peter Cushing, Gough and Miss Stribling with Christopher Lee as Dracula. *(Still 6820-13)*

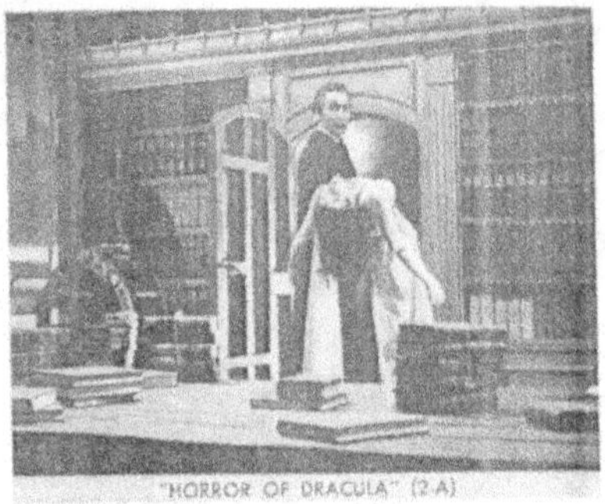

"HORROR OF DRACULA" (2-A)

THE MONSTER Dracula (Christopher Lee) abducts the vampire woman (Valerie Gaunt) from the castle library in this scene from "Horror of Dracula," based on Bram Stoker's horror classic. The new Hammer Film Productions, Ltd. Technicolor film being released by Universal-International stars Peter Cushing, Michael Gough and Melissa Stribling with Christopher Lee as Dracula. *(Still 6820-5)*

Christopher Lee, Master of Monsters, Puts New Horror Into 'Horror of Dracula'

(Advance)

When it comes to the ghoulish, the ghostly and the grisly, that's where Christopher Lee shines, cinematically speaking. The English film star, who has made an enviable reputation as a harbinger of horror, will next be seen as the unforgettable human vampire of Bram Stoker's famed novel in "Horror of Dracula," a new Technicolor motion picture from Hammer Film Productions, Ltd., scheduled to open next .... at the .... Theatre.

The picture, a Universal-International release, stars Peter Cushing, Michael Gough and Melissa Stribling, with Lee featured as Dracula.

Not too long ago Lee was acclaimed for his triumph of terror in the role of the repulsive monster of "The Curse of Frankenstein," a role in which he had to undergo three hours making up every day just to be fitted with the gruesome deaths-head he wore in the picture.

In "The Horror of Dracula," Lee's major cosmetic change is the pair of highly elongated canine teeth, normal attributes of a blood-sucking monster. As Count Dracula, Lee portrays an "undead" fiend who exists over the centuries on the blood of living humans. Cushing, creator of the monster in "The Curse of Frankenstein," portrays Van Helsing, the Dutch doctor who hunts Dracula down in an effort to end his reign of terror.

The same producer-writer-director team responsible for "The Curse of Frankenstein" was at the helm in producing "Horror of Dracula." Anthony Hinds was producer, Terence Fisher was director and Jimmy Sangster turned out the screenplay of both pictures.

Michael Carreras was executive producer and Anthony Nelson-Keys associate producer of "Horror of Dracula."

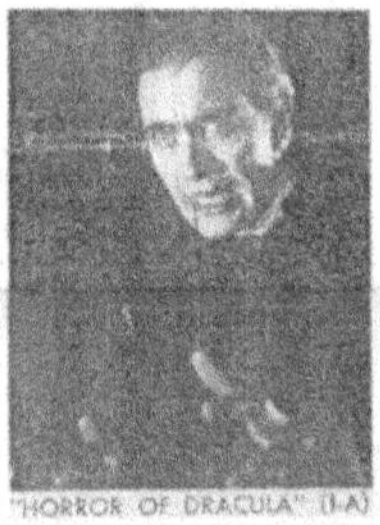

"HORROR OF DRACULA" (1-A)

CHRISTOPHER LEE in character for his classic role as the human vampire Dracula, in the new Hammer Film Productions, Ltd. Technicolor film based on the Bram Stoker shock classic. The Universal-International release stars Peter Cushing, Michael Gough and Melissa Stribling, with Lee featured as Dracula. *(Still 6820-4AD)*

'Dracula' Novel A Shocker For 50 Years

(Current)

The new Technicolor production of "Horror of Dracula," now at the .... Theatre, is based on the classic novel that has continued to shock the world for almost half a century. Bram Stoker's novel "Dracula," on which Hammer Film Productions, Ltd. based this Universal-International release, now at the .... Theatre, went on from its fabulously successful book form to curdle the blood in the veins of millions of playgoers when it was dramatized for the stage.

Many book editions have heavily enriched the Stoker family coffers as have film rights and play royalties. Stoker was considered a brilliant eccentric, a man who is said to have become a lawyer to escape jury service, an author who is said to have written one of the world's horror masterpieces following a hideous nightmare caused by overeating.

The new film production of this famous story of human vampires stars Peter Cushing, Michael Gough and Melissa Stribling with Christopher Lee as Dracula. Cushing and Lee were also starred in "The Curse of Frankenstein," which, like "Horror of Dracula," was produced by Anthony Hinds, directed by Terence Fisher and written as a screenplay by Jimmy Sangster.

'Frankenstein' Team Creates 'Dracula' Film

(Advance)

The acting combination and the producer - director - writer team which were responsible for the production of the widely acclaimed "The Curse of Frankenstein" are the creative talents at the helm of another of the all-time horror classics, "Horror of Dracula," which will open next .... at the .... Theatre.

This new Technicolor production based on the famous Bram Stoker novel was filmed by Hammer Film Productions, Ltd., for Universal-International release and stars Peter Cushing, Michael Gough and Melissa Stribling with Christopher Lee as Dracula.

Cushing was the master and Lee the monster in "The Curse of Frankenstein." Valerie Gaunt, an early victim of the vampire in "Horror of Dracula," was also an early victim of the monster in "The Curse of Frankenstein."

Producer Anthony Hinds, director Terence Fisher and screenplay writer Jimmy Sangster served in the same capacities in both pictures.

SELL IT BY SHRIEK, SHUDDER and **SHOCK** SHOWMANSHIP!!

SET OF TV SPOTS -- FREE!

All the weird horror and terrifying thrills experienced in "HORROR OF DRACULA" are expertly conveyed to potential box office patrons in a special set of television spots available Free to all exhibitors. These spots are designed to intrigue the lovers of shock and shudder screen stories. The set, all on 16mm film, includes one sixty-second and two twenty-second spots. These time spans include sufficient silent "tag" footage to allow for local theatre information. Order the set from JEFF LIVINGSTON, EASTERN ADVERTISING MANAGER, UNIVERSAL PICTURES CO., INC., 445 Park Avenue, New York 22, New York. In ordering, please specify the station or stations on which you plan to use the spots.

NIGHTMARE EFFECT FOR LOBBY

A coffin (or box), art work enlarged from Still No. 6820-EX 2D, horror copy along lines suggested above plus scads of eerie green lighting should attract the attention of the curious and lovers of the macabre. Order special art still FREE from Exploitation Dept., Universal Pictures, Inc., 445 Park Ave., New York 22, N.Y.

TV Telop or Slide

Both Telop and Slide are available as shown... $6.00 with theatre playdate and station identification information (to accompany order)... $5.00 without theatre playdate or station identification... $2.50 for each duplicate copy of any Telop or Slide. Be sure to mention whether you want Telop or Slide. Order direct from:

QQ TITLE CARD CO.
247 West 46th Street, New York, N. Y.

Suggested Audio Copy for Telop or Slide

"All new!... The great all-time shock-story!... See HORROR OF DRACULA!... but don't see it alone!... HORROR OF DRACULA!"

HERALDS STRESS HORROR!

Make Up Your Own!

Suggested here in tabloid form — ideal for distribution away from the theatre. Arrange the headline so the name of your town or city is used for more solid impact.

The above lay-out is based on Ad Mat No. 402. Order direct from National Screen Service.

Free Transcription

FOR SPOT RADIO USE. Available in FREE transcription form is a group of smash selling radio spots. All the drama, action and suspense found in the film is vividly captured for the benefit of radio listeners. The spots are 15, 30 and 60-second lengths and in every instance the time mentioned includes adequate opportunity for local playdate information to be given "live" by station announcer.

Order this FREE radio disc from RADIO DEPARTMENT, UNIVERSAL-INTERNATIONAL STUDIOS, UNIVERSAL CITY, CALIFORNIA

SUGGESTED COPY FOR LIVE RADIO SPOTS

(ONE MINUTE):
ANNOUNCER: "It's all new!... The great all-time shock-story... HORROR OF DRACULA!... The story of the terrifying lover who died — yet lived!... and of the women who, one by one, became the grisly dead-alive brides of Dracula!... HORROR OF DRACULA!... starring Peter Cushing!... Michael Gough!... Melissa Stribling!... with Christopher Lee as Dracula — the blood-lusting Dracula!... HORROR OF DRACULA!... by the creators of 'The Curse of Frankenstein'... HORROR OF DRACULA!... the unforgettable story of Count Dracula — who has been rising every night for 600 years from his coffin-bed — silently to seek the warm blood he needs to keep himself alive — and to turn each of his victims into a human vampire!... HORROR OF DRACULA!... but don't dare see it alone — the chill of the tomb won't leave your blood for hours!... HORROR OF DRACULA!... in Technicolor!"

(30-SECONDS):
ANNOUNCER: "It's all new — the great all-time shock-story — HORROR OF DRACULA!... the story of the terrifying lover who died — yet lived... and of the women who, one by one, became his grisly dead-alive brides!... HORROR OF DRACULA!... by the creators of 'The Curse of Frankenstein'!... See Peter Cushing, Michael Gough, Melissa Stribling with Christopher Lee as Dracula in HORROR OF DRACULA!... but don't dare see it alone!... HORROR OF DRACULA!... in Technicolor!"

(15-SECONDS):
ANNOUNCER: "See the all-new all-time shock-story — HORROR OF DRACULA!... by the creators of 'The Curse of Frankenstein'!... See HORROR OF DRACULA!... but don't dare see it alone!... HORROR OF DRACULA!... in Technicolor!"

SPECIAL FLAG AND BANNER ACCESSORIES
Order Direct From
National Flag Company
43 W. 21st St., New York 10, N.Y.
(In Canada: Order From Theatre Poster Service, 250 Victoria St., Toronto, Ont.)

SPECIAL KEY HORROR STILLS FOR NEWSPAPER IDENTIFICATION CONTEST -- OR -- 40 x 60 ADVANCE LOBBY POSTER

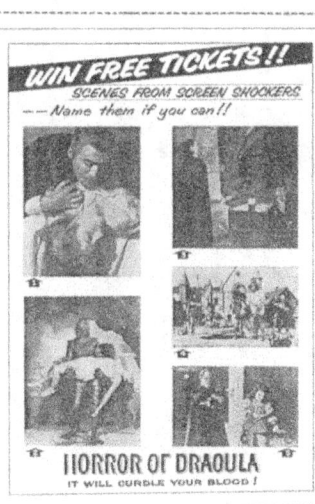

Order Set of Contest Stills FREE From EXPLOITATION DEPT., UNIVERSAL PICTURES, INC., 445 Park Avenue, New York 22, New York. No. 1, 682-22; No. 2, 1724-24A; No. 3 109-1132; No. 4, 1844-EX 17; No. 5, 1844-EX 16.

ANSWERS: 1. Horror of Dracula; 2. Creature From The Black Lagoon; 3. Dracula; 4. The Hunchback of Notre Dame; 5. The Phantom.

Heighten The Horror With Bold Ballyhoo

PREVIEW FOR ONE BRAVE WOMAN
Set this at midnight ... Invite the press or one feature story writer for reaction after screening.

STREET STUNT
Get old hearse ... place coffin inside and with appropriate banners and copy, route through downtown area.

NURSE IN LOBBY
At all times have a nurse in full uniform with first aid kit and hospital bed in attendance in the lobby.

TOMBSTONE
Erect or place a Tombstone outside the theatre. Suggested copy could be: Lovely Lucy lies here. "HORROR OF DRACULA" is indeed a Bloody Business.

BOOK and LIBRARY DISPLAYS
To feature all horror and science-fiction books, including Bram Stoker's "Dracula" suggest the use of green lights for dramatic effect.

SOUND EFFECTS
Everywhere possible — lobby front, sound truck, hearse, windows — use sound effects from the picture.

AMBULANCE OUT FRONT
NEVER fails to attract attention, particularly if a "man in white" walks into and out of theatre periodically.

WINDOWS
Take advantage of any empty windows to display scary advertising matter under a suffusion of green light.

SPIRIT OF DRACULA
Get tallest and handsomest man available — dress him in typical Dracula costume with flowing cape. Route him through busiest sections of your community and to colleges and high schools.

THRILL 'EM! CHILL 'EM! TEASE 'EM YOUR WAY!

Teaser Ad Mat No. 2A—75 Lines
2 col x 2½"

Teaser Ad Mat No. 1A—37 Lines
1 col x 2½"

Ad Mat No. 102—38 Lines
1 col x 2"

Ad Mat No. 202—70 Lines

Ad Mat No. 303—381 Lines
3 col x 9¼"

MR. SHOWMAN: If you are playing HORROR OF DRACULA and THE THING THAT COULDN'T DIE as a double program, here's how to make exciting, hard-selling combination ads. The ads reproduced below (in reduced sizes) were put together from the regular ads in the HORROR OF DRACULA and THE THING THAT COULDN'T DIE pressbooks.

Horror of Dracula Ad Mat No. 204
The Thing That Couldn't Die
Ad Mat No. 201
Approx. 146 Lines

Horror of Dracula Ad Mat No. 206
The Thing That Couldn't Die
Ad Mat No. 202
Approx. 235 Lines

Horror of Dracula Ad Mat No. 303
The Thing That Couldn't Die Ad Mat No. 303
Approx. 456 Lines

Horror of Dracula Ad Mat No. 102
The Thing That Couldn't Die Ad Mat No. 101
Approx. 45 Lines

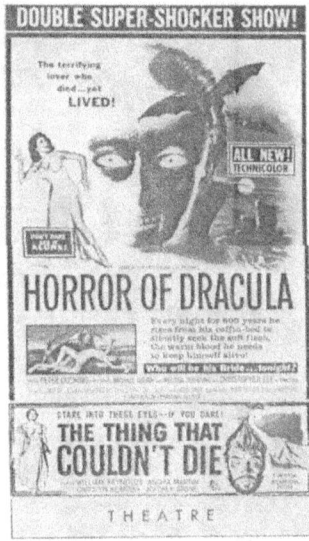

Horror of Dracula Ad Mat No. 302→
The Thing that Couldn't Die Ad Mat No. 302→
Approx. 378 Lines→

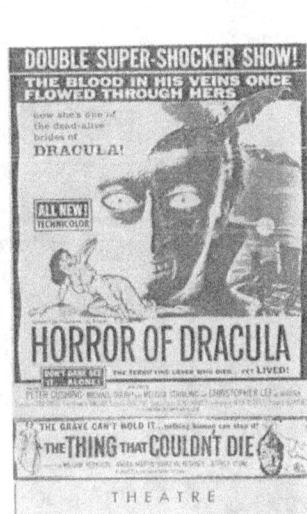

←Horror of Dracula Ad Mat No. 301
←The Thing That Couldn't Die Ad Mat No. 301
←Approx. 330 Lines

Horror of Dracula Ad Mat No. 207
The Thing That Couldn't Die
Ad Mat No. 203
Approx. 360 Lines

TV TELOP OR SLIDE

Both Telop and Slide are available as shown here ... $6.00 with theatre playdate and station identification information (to accompany order) ... $5.00 without theatre playdate and station identification ... $2.50 for each duplicate copy of any Telop or Slide. Be sure to mention whether you want TELOP or SLIDE. Order direct from ... QQ TITLE CARD CO., 247 WEST 46th ST., NEW YORK, N. Y.

"LIVE" COPY TO GO WITH TELOP OR SLIDE:

"See the great combination twin-terror show! ... HORROR OF DRACULA! ... by the creators of THE CURSE OF FRANKENSTEIN! ... Plus THE THING THAT COULDN'T DIE! ... Both on the same show!"

Suggested Copy For Live Radio Announcements:

(ONE MINUTE):

ANNOUNCER: "Here are spine-chilling thrills from the living dead! ... See this unbeatable all-new twin-terror combination show! ... HORROR OF DRACULA Plus THE THING THAT COULDN'T DIE ... HORROR OF DRACULA! ... the new shock-adventures of the terrifying lover who died — yet lived! ... and of the women who, one by one, became his dead-alive brides ... HORROR OF DRACULA! ... by the creators of THE CURSE OF FRANKENSTEIN! ... starring Peter Cushing, Michael Gough, Melissa Stribling — with Christopher Lee as Dracula! ... See it — but don't dare see it alone — the chill of the tomb won't leave your blood! ... HORROR OF DRACULA! ... Plus this co-headline horror-hit ... THE THING THAT COULDN'T DIE! ... the 400-year-old monster who rose from his grave to enslave every woman, overpower every man who dared stare into his eyes! ... See HORROR OF DRACULA in Technicolor ... and THE THING THAT COULDN'T DIE! ... Both on the one double-chill, double-thrill horror program!"

(30-SECONDS):

ANNOUNCER: "See this all new double-chill, double-thrill combination horror show! ... HORROR OF DRACULA Plus THE THING THAT COULDN'T DIE! ... HORROR OF DRACULA, by the creators of THE CURSE OF FRANKENSTEIN, the new shock-adventure of the terrifying lover who died — yet lived — and of the women who became his dead-alive brides! ... HORROR OF DRACULA Plus THE THING THAT COULDN'T DIE! ... the most terrifying monster that ever stalked the earth! ... See HORROR OF DRACULA in Technicolor and THE THING THAT COULDN'T DIE on the same twin-terror program!"

(15-SECONDS):

ANNOUNCER: "See two new terror-thrillers on one double-shock show! ... HORROR OF DRACULA, the all-time suspense adventure — in Technicolor! ... Plus THE THING THAT COULDN'T DIE! ... Both on the same chilling, thrilling program!"

NOTICE— There are also TWO recorded radio spots on the combination program for your convenience. You will find these spots on the REVERSE side of the transcription for "HORROR OF DRACULA." They are 60 seconds and 30 seconds in length, including time for live theatre tag by local announcer.

Special Composite Mat
EVERYTHING YOU NEED FOR A COMPLETE CAMPAIGN, ALL ON ONE MAT

MAT No. 206

Ad Mat No. 206   2 Col. x 7"—196 Lines

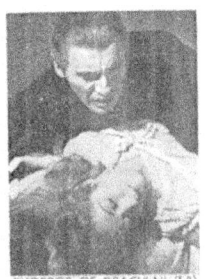
"HORROR OF DRACULA" (1-B)

"HORROR OF DRACULA" (2-A)

MAT No. 101

Ad Mat No. 101   1 Col. x 1"—14 Lines

MAT No. 201

Ad Mat No. 201—2 Col. x 1"—28 Lines

MAT No. 203

Ad Mat No. 203   2 Col. x 3"—84 Lines

SPECIAL MAT NO. 1   ORDER BY NAME AND NUMBER FROM NATIONAL SCREEN SERVICE

INDIVIDUAL MATS PICTURED ABOVE MAY BE ORDERED SINGLY (By number, indicated) AT THE REGULAR PRICE!

ACCESSORIES

THREE SHEET

TEASER SIX SHEET

14 x 36

ONE SHEET

22 x 28

WINDOW CARD

Order Trailer, Slide, Ad Scene Mats, Color Gloss Stills and Other Accessories from Your Local National Screen Service Exchange

UTILITY MAT NO. 1

British quad-poster with the original title

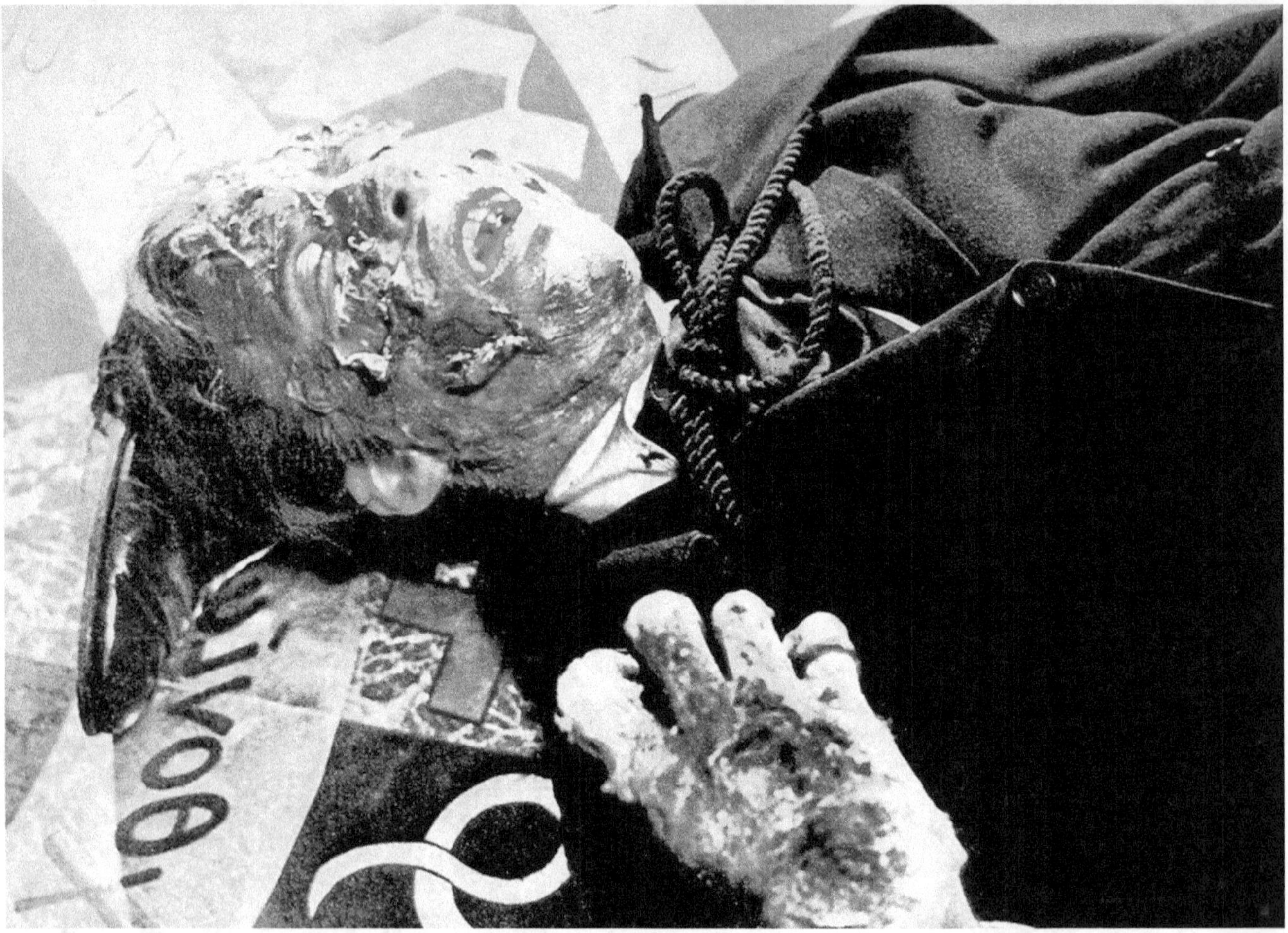

A scene from the uncensored Japanese version - thought too gruesome for English and American audiences

Background on John Polidori's "The Vampyre" by Michael Hartley

Dr John Polidori

In the fight for Italian unification many patriots were forced to seek political asylum in other countries, England being a popular choice. Gabriele Rossetti was one of these émigrés; he arrived in London in 1824 and took a position as professor of by Italian at King's College. He married Frances Polidori, the daughter of another Italian émigré, Gaetano Polidori, and they had four children; Maria, Dante Gabriel, William Michael and Christina. The Rossetti surname came from an earlier family nickname, on account of the distinctive red hair of the family.

Frances was the sister of John Polidori; born in London in 1795, he was educated at the Roman Catholic College of Ampleforth, Yorkshire, studied medicine at Edinburgh and received his by degree in 1815 (interestingly, considering what is to follow, his dissertation was on the subject of *Oneirodynia*, or nightmares, and at this time he also wrote an *Essay on the Punishment of Death*, a condemnation of suicide).

Lord Byron

The following year he took the position of personal physician to Lord George Gordon Byron, and was commissioned by the publisher John Murray, for a fee of £500, to write a diary of their by European travels, (later edited by his nephew, William Michael). This diary takes two forms; the first are personal notes and aides-mémoire, possibly intended to be expanded later, the second are definite, expansive descriptions (probably written with an eye on Murray's £500).

Villa Diodati

In June 1816, Byron and Polidori arrived at the Villa Diodati, on the shore of Lake Geneva, Switzerland, where they were joined by Percy Bysshe Shelley, Mary Wollstonecraft Godwin (Shelley's future wife), and Miss Claire Clairmont (with whom Byron would later have an affair). The summer of 1816 was extremely stormy and wet (the infamous *Summer That Never Was*) – on June 13th, Polidori recorded that he was returning back from a ball in a thunder and lightning storm and lost his way, on June 15th, attempting to jump a wall to aid Mary Godwin, he slipped on the wet ground and sprained his left ankle.

Mary Wollstonecraft Godwin

The "*wet, ungenial summer and incessant rainfall*" confined the party for days in the house, where they took to relating eerie stories and read aloud from *Fantasmagoriana* a French collection of horror stories (later translated into English as *Tales of the Dead* by Mrs Sarah Utterson).

On the evening of June 17th, they told more ghost stories and Byron recited lines from Coleridge's Christabel, whereupon, in the ensuing silence, Shelley suddenly screeched, threw his hands to his head and ran from the room – Polidori threw water on his face and gave him ether. He claimed to have seen a vision of a woman with eyes instead of nipples, which had horrified him.

Byron then proposed, *"We will each write a ghost-story,"* and Polidori began his the following day, a story about a skull-headed woman which he abandoned soon after and began again, taking his subject from a suggestion from Byron, who also had second thoughts and began again on a different subject.

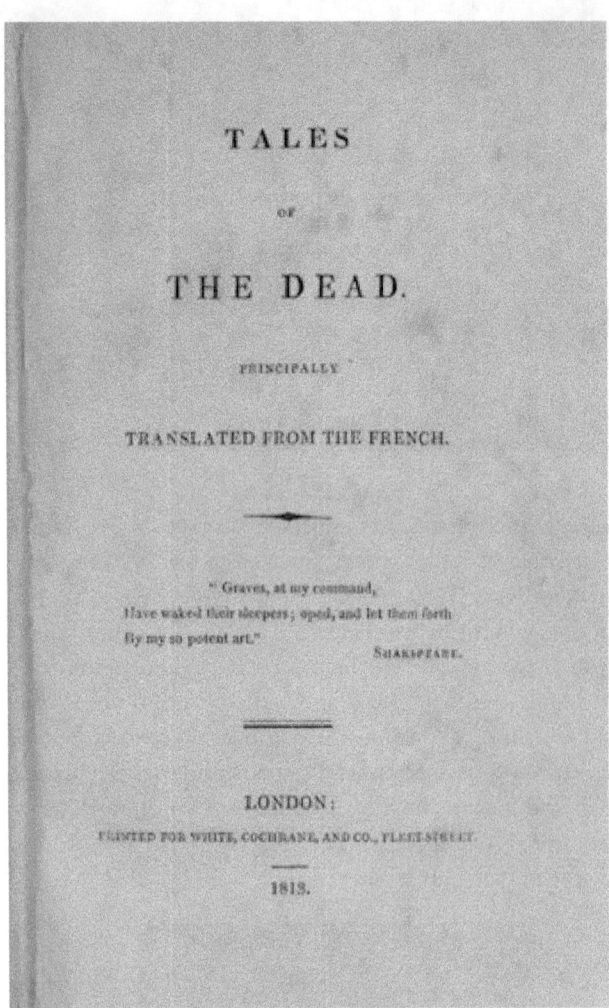

Sarah Utterson - Tales of the Dead - 1813

Claire Clairmont

Over the next three days they worked on their stories, although Shelley and Miss Clairmont did not finish theirs; Byron's tale was later published as a *Fragment of a Novel* as a postscript to his poem *Mazzepa*. Mary Wollstonecraft Shelley published her story as a three-volume novel, in an edition of 500 copies, on January 1st 1818, entitled *Frankenstein, or The Modern Prometheus*.

Polidori's story was published in 1819 without his permission, and attributed to Lord Byron, in the *New Monthly Magazine* as *The Vampyre*. It was the first romantic vampire novel, and was an immediate success (not least to the name of Byron being associated it. Byron was immensely popular at the time – the equivalent to a rock star (think Elvis) in our day, and the confusion was heightened as the main character of *The Vampyre* is Lord Ruthven, the name of a thinly-disguised portrayal of Byron in Lady Caroline Lamb's novel *Glenarvon*).

Percy Shelley

Frontispiece - Mary Shelley - Frankenstein - 1831 Edition

Early depiction of a female vampire

When Polidori and Byron parted company later in 1816 (on the grounds, as Polidori put it, *'not upon any quarrel, but on account of our not suiting'*), he left the manuscript with the Countess of Breuss, but an unnamed traveller obtained it and it passed into the hands of the publisher, Colburn. It appeared in the *New Monthly Magazine* on April 1st 1819, but an edition in book form was registered at Stationer's Hall on March 27th 1819, by Sherwood, Neely and Jones. Polidori wrote to both publishers, demanding an explanation, that Byron's name be removed from the work and his own used instead, and for compensation. *The Vampyre* sparked a vampire revolution in literature; at least three vampire operas appeared in the 19th century, Tolstoy, Gogol and Dumas wrote vampire stories of their own, Burton published *Vikram and the Vampire*, Kipling wrote a poem *The Vampire* and Polidori's tale was the obvious precursor of that quintessential vampire novel, Bram Stoker's *Dracula* (1897). The interest and popularity of the vampire has never diminished – witness today's *Buffy* or *Twilight* series, and the myriad vampire films, novels and websites that continue to be produced (for better or for worse).

Polidori's health began to worsen following his rift with Byron, he became depressed and started to gamble. On August 24th 1821, he went to bed and drank a draught of prussic acid (cyanide), dying instantly.

There have been differing accounts of his death but his nephew, William Michael Rossetti, in his introduction to Polidori's *Diary*, wrote,

"That he did take poison, prussic acid, was a fact perfectly well known in his family; but it is curious to note that the easy-going and good-naturedly disposed coroner's jury were content to return a verdict without eliciting any distinct evidence as to the cause of death, and they simply pronounced that he had " died by the visitation of God,"

An ironic end considering his *Essay on the Punishment of Death* from five years previous, in which examined and condemned the practice of suicide. His sister, Charlotte, transcribed his unpublished *Diary* and removed certain *'peccant passages'* before destroying the original. Rossetti's edition appeared in 1911.

William Michael Rossetti

THE

VAMPYRE;

A Tale.

LONDON:

PRINTED FOR SHERWOOD, NEELY, AND JONES,

PATERNOSTER-ROW.

—

1819.

[Entered at Stationers' Hall, March 27, 1819.]

THE VAMPYRE
by
John Polidori
1819
The Complete Text to the Original Gothic Vampire Story

It happened that in the midst of the dissipations attendant upon London winter, there appeared at the various parties of the leaders of the ton a nobleman more remarkable for his singularities, than his rank. He gazed upon the mirth around him, as if he could not participate therein. Apparently, the light laughter of the fair only attracted his attention, that he might by a look quell it and throw fear into those breasts where thoughtlessness reigned.

Those who felt this sensation of awe, could not explain whence it arose: some attributed it to the dead grey eye, which, fixing upon the object's face, did not seem to penetrate, and at one glance to pierce through to the inward workings of the heart; but fell upon the cheek with a leaden ray that weighed upon the skin it could not pass. His peculiarities caused him to be invited to every house; all wished to see him, and those who had been accustomed to violent excitement, and now felt the weight of ennui, were pleased at having something in their presence capable of engaging their attention.

In spite of the deadly hue of his face, which never gained a wanner tint, either from the blush of modesty, or from the strong emotion of passion, though its form and outline were beautiful, many of the female hunters after notoriety attempted to win his attentions, and gain, at least, some marks of what they might term affection: Lady Mercer, who had been the mockery of every monster shewn in drawing-rooms since her marriage, threw herself in his way, and did all but put on the dress of a mountebank, to attract his notice -- though in vain; -- when she stood before him, though his eyes were apparently fixed upon hers, still it seemed as if they were unperceived; -- even her unappalled impudence was baffled, and she left the field. But though the common adultress could not influence even the guidance of his eyes, it was not that the female sex was indifferent to him: yet such was the apparent caution with which he spoke to the virtuous wife and innocent daughter, that few knew he ever addressed himself to females. He had, however, the reputation of a winning tongue; and whether it was that it even overcame the dread of his singular character, or that they were moved by his apparent hatred of vice, he was as often among those females who form the boast of their sex from their domestic virtues, as among those who sully it by their vices.

About the same time, there came to London a young gentleman of the name of Aubrey: he was an orphan left with an only sister in the possession of great wealth, by parents who died while he was yet in childhood. Left also to himself by guardians, who thought it their duty merely to take care of his fortune, while they relinquished the more important charge of his mind to the care of mercenary subalterns, he cultivated more his imagination than his judgment.

He had, hence, that high romantic feeling of honour and candour, which daily ruins so many milliners' apprentices. He believed all to sympathise with virtue, and thought that vice was thrown in by Providence merely for the picturesque effect of the scene, as we see in romances: he thought that the misery of a cottage merely consisted in the vesting of clothes, which were as warm, but which were better adapted to the painter's eye by their irregular folds and various coloured patches.

He thought, in fine, that the dreams of poets were the realities of life. He was handsome, frank, and rich: for these reasons, upon his entering into the gay circles, many mothers surrounded him, striving which should describe with least truth their languishing or romping favourites: the daughters at the same time, by their brightening countenances when he approached, and by their sparkling eyes, when he opened his lips, soon led him into false notions of his talents and his merit. Attached as he was to the romance of his solitary hours, he was startled at finding, that, except in the tallow and wax candles that flickered, not from the presence of a ghost, but from want of snuffing, there was no foundation in real life for any of that congeries of pleasing pictures and descriptions contained in those volumes, from which he had formed his study. Finding, however, some compensation in his gratified vanity, he was about to relinquish his dreams, when the extraordinary being we have above described, crossed him in his career.

He watched him; and the very impossibility of forming an idea of the character of a man entirely absorbed in himself, who gave few other signs of his observation of external objects, than the tacit assent to their existence, implied by the avoidance of their contact: allowing his imagination to picture every thing that flattered its propensity to extravagant ideas, he soon formed this object into the hero of a romance, and determined to observe the offspring of his fancy, rather than the person before him. He became acquainted with him, paid him attentions, and so far advanced upon his notice, that his presence was always recognised. He gradually learnt that Lord Ruthven's affairs were embarrassed, and soon found, from the notes of preparation in ---- Street, that he was about to travel.

Desirous of gaining some information respecting this singular character, who, till now, had only whetted his curiosity, he hinted to his guardians, that it was time for him to perform the tour, which for many generations has been thought necessary to enable the young to take some rapid steps in the career of vice towards putting themselves upon an equality with the aged, and not allowing them to appear as if fallen from the skies, whenever scandalous intrigues are mentioned as the subjects of pleasantry or of praise, according to the degree of skill shewn in carrying them on. They consented: and Aubrey immediately mentioning his intentions to Lord Ruthven, was surprised to receive from him a proposal to join him. Flattered such a mark of esteem from him, who, apparently, had nothing in common with other men, he gladly accepted it, and in a few days they had passed the circling waters.

Hitherto, Aubrey had had no opportunity of studying Lord Ruthven's character, and now he found, that, though many more of his actions were exposed to his view, the results offered different conclusions from the apparent motives to his conduct. His companion was profuse in his liberality; -- the idle, the vagabond, and the beggar, received from his hand more than enough to relieve their immediate wants. But Aubrey could not avoid remarking, that it was not upon the virtuous, reduced to indigence by the misfortunes attendant even upon virtue, that he bestowed his alms; -- these were sent from the door with hardly suppressed sneers; but when the profligate came to ask something, not to relieve his wants, but to allow him to wallow in his lust, to sink him still deeper in his iniquity, he was sent away with rich charity. This was, however, attributed by him to the greater importunity of the vicious, which generally prevails over the retiring bashfulness of the virtuous indigent.

There was one circumstance about the charity of his Lordship, which was still more impressed upon his mind: all those upon whom it was bestowed, inevitably found that there was a curse upon it, for they were all either led to the scaffold, or sunk to the lowest and the most abject misery. At Brussels and other towns through which they passed, Aubrey was surprised at the apparent eagerness with which his companion sought for the centres of all fashionable vice; there he entered into all the spirit of the faro table: he betted and always gambled with success, except where the known sharper was his antagonist, and then he lost even more than he gained; but it was always with the same unchanging face, with which he generally watched the society around: it was not, however, so when he encountered the rash youthful novice, or the luckless father of a numerous family; then his very wish seemed fortune's law -- this apparent abstractedness of mind was laid aside, and his eyes sparkled with more fire than that of the cat whilst dallying with the half-dead mouse.

In every town, he left the formerly affluent youth, torn from the circle he adorned, cursing, in the solitude of a dungeon, the fate that had drawn him within the reach of this fiend; whilst many a father sat frantic, amidst the speaking looks of mute hungry children, without a single farthing of his late immense wealth, wherewith to buy even sufficient to satisfy their present craving. Yet he took no money from the gambling table; but immediately lost, to the ruiner of many, the last gilder he had just snatched from the convulsive grasp of the innocent: this might but be the result of a certain degree of knowledge, which was not, however, capable of combating the cunning of the more experienced. Aubrey often wished to represent this to his friend, and beg him to resign that charity and pleasure which proved the ruin of all, and did not tend to his own profit; but he delayed it -- for each day he hoped his friend would give him some opportunity of speaking frankly and openly to him; however, this never occurred. Lord Ruthven in his carriage, and amidst the various wild and rich scenes of nature, was always the same: his eye spoke less than his lip; and though Aubrey was near the object of his curiosity, he obtained no greater gratification from it than the constant excitement of vainly wishing to break that mystery, which to his exalted imagination began to assume the appearance of something supernatural.

They soon arrived at Rome, and Aubrey for a time lost sight of his companion; he left him in daily attendance upon the morning circle of an Italian countess, whilst he went in search of the memorials of another almost deserted city. Whilst he was thus engaged, letters arrived from England, which he opened with eager impatience; the first was from his sister, breathing nothing but affection; the others were from his guardians, the latter astonished him; if it had before entered into his imagination that there was an evil power resident in his companion these seemed to give him almost sufficient reason for the belief. His guardians insisted upon his immediately leaving his friend, and urged that his character was dreadfully vicious, for that the possession of irresistible powers of seduction, rendered his licentious habits more dangerous to society. It had been discovered, that his contempt for the adultress had not originated in hatred of her character; but that he had required, to enhance his gratification, that his victim, the partner of his guilt, should be hurled from the pinnacle of unsullied virtue, down to the lowest abyss of infamy and degradation: in fine, that all those females whom he had sought, apparently on account of their virtue, had, since his departure, thrown even the mask aside, and had not scrupled to expose the whole deformity of their vices to the public gaze.

Aubrey determined upon leaving one, whose character had not shown a single bright point on which to rest the eye. He resolved to invent some plausible pretext for abandoning him altogether, purposing, in the mean while, to watch him more closely, and to let no slight circumstances pass by unnoticed. He entered into the same circle, and soon perceived, that his Lordship was endeavouring to work upon the inexperience of the daughter of the lady whose house he chiefly frequented. In Italy, it is seldom that an unmarried female is met with in society; he was therefore obliged to carry on his plans in secret; but Aubrey's eye followed him in all his windings, and soon discovered that an assignation had been appointed, which would most likely end in the ruin of an innocent, though thoughtless girl.

Losing no time, he entered the apartment of Lord Ruthven, and abruptly asked him his intentions with respect to the lady, informing him at the same time that he was aware of his being about to meet her that very night. Lord Ruthven answered, that his intentions were such as he supposed all would have upon such an occasion; and upon being pressed whether he intended to marry her, merely laughed. Aubrey retired; and, immediately writing a note, to say, that from that moment he must decline accompanying his Lordship in the remainder of their proposed tour, he ordered his servant to seek other apartments, and calling upon the mother of the lady informed her of all he knew, not only with regard to her daughter, but also concerning the character of his Lordship. The assignation was prevented. Lord Ruthven next day merely sent his servant to notify his complete assent to a separation; but did not hint any suspicion of his plans having been foiled by Aubrey's interposition.

Having left Rome, Aubrey directed his steps towards Greece, and crossing the Peninsula, soon found himself at Athens. He then fixed residence in the house of a Greek; and soon occupied himself in tracing the faded records of ancient glory upon monuments that apparently, ashamed of chronicling the deeds of freemen only before slaves, had hidden themselves beneath the sheltering soil or many coloured lichen. Under the same roof as himself, existed a being, so beautiful and delicate, that she might have formed the model for a painter, wishing to portray on canvass the promised hope of the faithful in Mahomet's paradise, save that her eyes spoke too much mind for any one to think she could belong to those who had no souls. As she danced upon the plain, or tripped along the mountain's side, one would have thought the gazelle a poor type of her beauties; for who would have exchanged her eye, apparently the eye of animated nature, for that sleepy luxurious look of the animal suited but to the taste of an epicure. The light step of Ianthe often accompanied Aubrey in his search after antiquities, and often would the unconscious girl, engaged in the pursuit of a Kashmere butterfly, show the whole beauty of her form, floating as it were upon the wind, to the eager gaze of him, who forgot the letters he had just decyphered upon an almost effaced tablet, in the contemplation of her sylph-like figure.

Often would her tresses falling, as she flitted around, exhibit in the sun's ray such delicately brilliant and swiftly fading hues, as might well excuse the forgetfulness of the antiquary, who let escape from his mind the very object he had before thought of vital importance to the proper interpretation of a passage in Pausanias. But why attempt to describe charms which all feel, but none can appreciate? -- It was innocence, youth, and beauty, unaffected by crowded drawing-rooms and stifling balls. Whilst he drew those remains of which he wished to preserve a memorial for his future hours, she would stand by, and watch the magic effects of his pencil, in tracing the scenes of her native place; she would then describe to him the circling dance upon the open plain, would paint to him in all the glowing colours of youthful memory, the marriage pomp she remembered viewing in her infancy; and then, turning to subjects that had evidently made a greater impression upon her mind, would tell him all the supernatural tales of her nurse.

Her earnestness and apparent belief of what she narrated, excited the interest even of Aubrey; and often as she told him the tale of the living vampyre, who had passed years amidst his friends, and dearest ties, forced every year, by feeding upon the life of a lovely female to prolong his existence for the ensuing months, his blood would run cold, whilst he attempted to laugh her out of such idle and horrible fantasies; but Ianthe cited to him the names of old men, who had at last detected one living among themselves, after several of their near relatives and children had been found marked with the stamp of the fiend's appetite; and when she found him so incredulous, she begged of him to believe her, for it had been remarked, that those who had dared to question their existence, always had some proof given, which obliged them, with grief and heartbreaking, to confess it was true. She detailed to him the traditional appearance of these monsters, and his horror was increased by hearing a pretty accurate description of Lord Ruthven; he, however, still persisted in persuading her, that there could be no truth in her fears, though at the same time he wondered at the many coincidences which had all tended to excite a belief in the supernatural power of Lord Ruthven.

Aubrey began to attach himself more and more to Ianthe; her innocence, so contrasted with all the affected virtues of the women among whom he had sought for his vision of romance, won his heart and while he ridiculed the idea of a young man of English habits, marrying an uneducated Greek girl, still he found himself more and more attached to the almost fairy form before him. He would tear himself at times from her, and, forming a plan for some antiquarian research, would depart, determined not to return until his object was attained; but he always found it impossible to fix his attention upon the ruins around him, whilst in his mind he retained an image that seemed alone the rightful possessor of his thoughts. Ianthe was unconscious of his love, and was ever the same frank infantile being he had first known.

She always seemed to part from him with reluctance; but it was because she had no longer any one with whom she could visit her favourite haunts, whilst her guardian was occupied in sketching or uncovering some fragment which had yet escaped the destructive hand of time. She had appealed to her parents on the subject of Vampyres, and they both, with several present, affirmed their existence, pale with horror at the very name. Soon after, Aubrey determined to proceed upon one of his excursions, which was to detain him for a few hours; when they heard the name of the place, they all at once begged of him not to return at night, as he must necessarily pass through a wood, where no Greek would ever remain, after the day had closed, upon any consideration. They described it as the resort of the vampyres in their nocturnal orgies and denounced the most heavy evils as impending upon him who dared to cross their path. Aubrey made light of their representations, and tried to laugh them out of the idea; but when he saw them shudder at his daring thus to mock a superior, infernal power, the very name of which apparently made their blood freeze, he was silent.

Next morning Aubrey set off upon his excursion unattended; he was surprised to observe the melancholy face of his host, and was concerned to find that his words, mocking the belief of those horrible fiends, had inspired them with such terror. When he was about to depart, Ianthe came to the side of his horse, and earnestly begged of him to return, ere night allowed the power of these beings to be put in action; -- he promised. He was, however, so occupied in his research, that he did not perceive that day-light would soon end, and that in the horizon there was one of those specks which, in the warmer climates, so rapidly gather into a tremendous mass, and pour all their rage upon the devoted country. -- He at last, however, mounted his horse, determined to make up by speed for his delay: but it was too late. Twilight, in these southern climates, is almost unknown; immediately the sun sets, night begins: and ere he had advanced far, the power of the storm was above -- its echoing thunders had scarcely an interval of rest; -- its thick heavy rain forced its way through the canopying foliage, whilst the blue forked lightning seemed to fall and radiate at his very feet. Suddenly his horse took fright, and he was carried with dreadful rapidity through the entangled forest.

The animal at last, through fatigue, stopped, and he found, by the glare of lightning, that he was in the neighbourhood of a hovel that hardly lifted itself up from the masses of dead leaves and brushwood which surrounded it. Dismounting, he approached, hoping to find some one to guide him to the town, or at least trusting to obtain shelter from the pelting of the storm. As he approached, the thunders, for a moment silent, allowed him to hear the dreadful shrieks of a woman mingling with the stifled, exultant mockery of a laugh, continued in one almost unbroken sound; -- he was startled: but, roused by the thunder which again rolled over his head, he, with a sudden effort, forced open the door of the hut. He found himself in utter darkness: the sound, however, guided him. He was apparently unperceived; for, though he called, still the sounds continued, and no notice was taken of him. He found himself in contact with some one, whom he immediately seized; when a voice cried, "Again baffled!" to which a loud laugh succeeded; and he felt himself grappled by one whose strength seemed superhuman: determined to sell his life as dearly as he could, he struggled; but it was in vain: he was lifted from his feet and hurled with enormous force against the ground: -- his enemy threw himself upon him, and kneeling upon his breast, had placed his hands upon his throat when the glare of many torches penetrating through the hole that gave light in the day, disturbed him; -- he instantly rose, and, leaving his prey, rushed through the door, and in a moment the crashing of branches, as he broke through the wood, was no longer heard.

The storm was now still; and Aubrey, incapable of moving, was soon heard by those without. They entered; the light of their torches fell upon mud walls, and the thatch loaded on every individual straw with heavy flakes of soot. At the desire of Aubrey they searched for her who had attracted him by her cries; he was again left in darkness; but what was his horror, when the light of the torches once more burst upon him, to perceive the airy form of his fair conductress brought in a lifeless corpse. He shut his eyes, hoping that it was but a vision arising from his disturbed imagination; but he again saw the same form, when he unclosed them, stretched by his side.

There was no colour upon her cheek, not even upon her lip; yet there was a stillness about her face that seemed almost as attaching as the life that once dwelt there: -- upon her neck and breast was blood, and upon her throat were the marks of teeth having opened the vein: -- to this the men pointed, crying, simultaneously struck with horror, "A Vampyre! a Vampyre!" A litter was quickly formed, and Aubrey was laid by the side of her who had lately been to him the object of so many bright and fairy visions, now fallen; with the flower of life that had died within her. He knew not what his thoughts were -- his mind was benumbed and seemed to shun reflection and take refuge in vacancy; -- he held almost unconsciously in his hand a naked dagger of a particular construction, which had been found in the hut.

They were soon met by different parties who had been engaged in the search of her whom a mother had missed. Their lamentable cries as they approached the city, forewarned the parents of some dreadful catastrophe. -- To describe their grief would be impossible; but when they ascertained the cause of their child's death, they looked at Aubrey and pointed to the corpse. They were inconsolable; both died brokenhearted.

Aubrey being put to bed was seized with a most violent fever, and was often delirious; in these intervals he would call upon Lord Ruthven and upon Ianthe -- by some unaccountable combination he seemed to beg of his former companion to spare the being he loved. At other times he would imprecate maledictions upon his head, and curse him as her destroyer.

Lord Ruthven chanced at this time to arrive at Athens, and from whatever motive, upon hearing of the state of Aubrey, immediately placed himself in the same house, and became his constant attendant. When the latter recovered from his delirium, he was horrified and startled at the sight of him whose image he had now combined with that of a Vampyre; but Lord Ruthven, by his kind words, implying almost repentance for the fault that had caused their separation, and still more by the attention, anxiety, and care which he showed, soon reconciled him to his presence.

His lordship seemed quite changed; he no longer appeared that apathetic being who had so astonished Aubrey; but as soon as his convalescence began to be rapid, he again gradually retired into the same state of mind, and Aubrey perceived no difference from the former man, except that at times he was surprised to meet his gaze fixed intently upon him, with a smile of malicious exultation playing upon his lips: he knew not why, but this smile haunted him. During the last stage of the invalid's recovery, Lord Ruthven was apparently engaged in watching the tideless waves raised by the cooling breeze, or in marking the progress of those orbs, circling, like our world, the moveless sun; -- indeed, he appeared to wish to avoid the eyes of all.

Aubrey's mind, by this shock, was much weakened, and that elasticity of spirit which had once so distinguished him now seemed to have fled for ever. He was now as much a lover of solitude and silence as Lord Ruthven; but much as he wished for solitude, his mind could not find it in the neighbourhood of Athens; if he sought it amidst the ruins he had formerly frequented, Ianthe's form stood by his side; -- if he sought it in the woods, her light step would appear wandering amidst the underwood, in quest of the modest violet; then suddenly turning round, would show, to his wild imagination, her pale face and wounded throat, with a meek smile upon her lips. He determined to fly scenes, every feature of which created such bitter associations in his mind. He proposed to Lord Ruthven, to whom he held himself bound by the tender care he had taken of him during his illness, that they should visit those parts of Greece neither had yet seen.

They travelled in every direction, and sought every spot to which a recollection could be attached: but though they thus hastened from place to place, yet they seemed not to heed what they gazed upon. They heard much of robbers, but they gradually began to slight these reports, which they imagined were only the invention of individuals, whose interest it was to excite the generosity of those whom they defended from pretended dangers. In consequence of thus neglecting the advice of the inhabitants, on one occasion they travelled with only a few guards, more to serve as guides than as a defence. Upon entering, however, a narrow defile, at the bottom of which was the bed of a torrent, with large masses of rock brought down from the neighbouring precipices, they had reason to repent their negligence; for scarcely were the whole of the party engaged in the narrow pass, when they were startled by the whistling of bullets close to their heads, and by the echoed report of several guns. In an instant their guards had left them, and, placing themselves behind rocks, had begun to fire in the direction whence the report came. Lord Ruthven and Aubrey, imitating their example, retired for a moment behind the sheltering turn of the defile: but ashamed of being thus detained by a foe, who with insulting shouts bade them advance, and being exposed to unresisting slaughter, if any of the robbers should climb above and take them in the rear, they determined at once to rush forward in search of the enemy. Hardly had they lost the shelter of rock, when Lord Ruthven received a shot in the shoulder, which brought him to the ground. Aubrey hastened to his assistance; and, no longer heeding the contest or his own peril, was soon surprised by seeing the robbers' faces around him -- his guards having, upon Lord Ruthven's being wounded, immediately thrown up their arms and surrendered.

By promises of great reward, Aubrey soon induced them to convey his wounded friend to a neighbouring cabin; and having agreed upon a ransom, he was no more disturbed by their presence -- they being content merely to guard the entrance till their comrade should return with the promised sum, for which he had an order. Lord Ruthven's strength rapidly decreased; in two days mortification ensued, and death seemed advancing with hasty steps.

His conduct and appearance had not changed; he seemed as unconscious of pain as he had been of the objects about him: but towards the close of the last evening, his mind became apparently uneasy, and his eye often fixed upon Aubrey, who was induced to offer his assistance with more than usual earnestness -- "Assist me! you may save me -- you may do more than that -- I mean not life, I heed the death of my existence as little as that of the passing day; but you may save my honour, your friend's honour." -- "How? tell me how? I would do any thing," replied Aubrey. -- "I need but little, my life ebbs apace -- I cannot explain the whole -- but if you would conceal all you know of me, my honour were free from stain in the world's mouth -- and if my death were unknown for some time in England -- I -- I -- but life." -- "It shall not be known." -- "Swear!" cried the dying man raising himself with exultant violence. "Swear by all your soul reveres, by all your nature fears, swear that for a year and a day you will not impart your knowledge of my crimes or death to any living being in any way, whatever may happen, or whatever you may see." -- His eyes seemed bursting from their sockets; "I swear!" said Aubrey; he sunk laughing upon his pillow, and breathed no more.

Aubrey retired to rest, but did not sleep; the many circumstances attending his acquaintance with this man rose upon his mind, and he knew not why; when he remembered his oath a cold shivering came over him, as if from the presentiment of something horrible awaiting him. Rising early in the morning, he was about to enter the hovel in which he had left the corpse, when a robber met him, and informed him that it was no longer there, having been conveyed by himself and comrades, upon his retiring, to the pinnacle of a neighbouring mount, according to a promise they had given his lordship, that it should be exposed to the first cold ray of the moon that rose after his death. Aubrey astonished, and taking several of the men, determined to go and bury it upon the spot where it lay. But, when he had mounted to the summit he found no trace of either the corpse or the clothes, though the robbers swore they pointed out the identical rock on which they had laid the body. For a time his mind was bewildered in conjectures, but he at last returned, convinced that they had buried the corpse for the sake of the clothes.

Weary of a country in which he had met with such terrible misfortunes, and in which all apparently conspired to heighten that superstitious melancholy that had seized upon his mind, he resolved to leave it, and soon arrived at Smyrna. While waiting for a vessel to convey him to Otranto, or to Naples, he occupied himself in arranging those effects he had with him belonging to Lord Ruthven. Amongst other things there was a case containing several weapons of offence, more or less adapted to ensure the death of the victim. There were several daggers and ataghans. Whilst turning them over, and examining their curious forms, what was his surprise at finding a sheath apparently ornamented in the same style as the dagger discovered in the fatal hut; -- he shuddered; hastening to gain further proof, he found the weapon, and his horror may be imagined when he discovered that it fitted, though peculiarly shaped, the sheath he held in his hand. His eyes seemed to need no further certainty -- they seemed gazing to be bound to the dagger, yet still he wished to disbelieve; but the particular form, the same varying tints upon the haft and sheath were alike in splendour on both, and left no room for doubt; there were also drops of blood on each.

He left Smyrna, and on his way home, at Rome, his first inquiries were concerning the lady he had attempted to snatch from Lord Ruthven's seductive arts. Her parents were in distress, their fortune ruined, and she had not been heard of since the departure of his lordship. Aubrey's mind became almost broken under so many repeated horrors; he was afraid that this lady had fallen a victim to the destroyer of Ianthe. He became morose and silent; and his only occupation consisted in urging the speed of the postilions, as if he were going to save the life of some one he held dear. He arrived at Calais; a breeze, which seemed obedient to his will, soon wafted him to the English shores; and he hastened to the mansion of his fathers, and there, for a moment, appeared to lose, in the embraces and caresses of his sister, all memory of the past. If she before, by her infantine caresses, had gained his affection, now that the woman began to appear, she was still more attaching as a companion.

Miss Aubrey had not that winning grace which gains the gaze and applause of the drawing-room assemblies. There was none of that light brilliancy which only exists in the heated atmosphere of a crowded apartment. Her blue eye was never lit up by the levity of the mind beneath. There was a melancholy charm about it which did not seem to arise from misfortune, but from some feeling within, that appeared to indicate a soul conscious of a brighter realm. Her step was not that light footing, which strays where'er a butterfly or a colour may attract -- it was sedate and pensive. When alone, her face was never brightened by the smile of joy; but when her brother breathed to her his affection, and would in her presence forget those griefs she knew destroyed his rest, who would have exchanged her smile for that of the voluptuary? It seemed as if those eyes, that face were then playing in the light of their own native sphere.

She was yet only eighteen, and had not been presented to the world, it having been thought by her guardians more fit that her presentation should be delayed until her brother's return from the continent, when he might be her protector. It was now, therefore, resolved that the next drawing-room, which was fast approaching, should be the epoch of her entry into the "busy scene." Aubrey would rather have remained in the mansion of his fathers, and feed upon the melancholy which overpowered him. He could not feel interest about the frivolities of fashionable strangers, when his mind had been so torn by the events he had witnessed; but he determined to sacrifice his own comfort to the protection of his sister. They soon arrived in town, and prepared for the next day, which had been announced as a drawing- room.

The crowd was excessive -- a drawing-room had not been held for long time, and all who were anxious to bask in the smile of royalty, hastened thither. Aubrey was there with his sister. While he was standing in a corner by himself, heedless of all around him, engaged in the remembrance that the first time he had seen Lord Ruthven was in that very place -- he felt himself suddenly seized by the arm, and a voice he recognized too well, sounded in his ear -- "Remember your oath." He had hardly courage to turn, fearful of seeing a spectre that would blast him, when he perceived, at a little distance, the same figure which had attracted his notice on this spot upon his first entry into society. He gazed till his limbs almost refusing to bear their weight, he was obliged to take the arm of a friend, and forcing a passage through the crowd, he threw himself into his carriage, and was driven home. He paced the room with hurried steps, and fixed his hands upon his head, as if he were afraid his thoughts were bursting from his brain. Lord Ruthven again before him -- circumstances started up in dreadful array -- the dagger -- his oath. -- He roused himself, he could not believe it possible -- the dead rise again! -- He thought his imagination had conjured up the image his mind was resting upon.

It was impossible that it could be real -- he determined, therefore, to go again into society; for though he attempted to ask concerning Lord Ruthven, the name hung upon his lips and he could not succeed in gaining information. He went a few nights after with his sister to the assembly of a near relation. Leaving her under the protection of a matron, he retired into a recess, and there gave himself up to his own devouring thoughts. Perceiving, at last, that many were leaving, he roused himself, and entering another room, found his sister surrounded by several, apparently in earnest conversation; he attempted to pass and get near her, when one, whom he requested to move, turned round, and revealed to him those features he most abhorred. He sprang forward, seized his sister's arm, and, with hurried step, forced her towards the street: at the door he found himself impeded by the crowd of servants who were waiting for their lords; and while he was engaged in passing them, he again heard that voice whisper close to him -- "Remember your oath!" -- He did not dare to turn, but, hurrying his sister, soon reached home.

Aubrey became almost distracted. If before his mind had been absorbed by one subject, how much more completely was it engrossed now that the certainty of the monster's living again pressed upon his thoughts. His sister's attentions were now unheeded, and it was in vain that she intreated him to explain to her what had caused his abrupt conduct. He only uttered a few words, and those terrified her. The more he thought, the more he was bewildered. His oath startled him; -- was he then to allow this monster to roam, bearing ruin upon his breath, amidst all he held dear, and not avert its progress? His very sister might have been touched by him. But even if he were to break his oath, and disclose his suspicions, who would believe him? He thought of employing his own hand to free the world from such a wretch; but death, he remembered, had been already mocked. For days he remained in state; shut up in his room, he saw no one, and ate only when his sister came, who, with eyes streaming with tears, besought him, for her sake, to support nature.

At last, no longer capable of bearing stillness and solitude, he left his house, roamed from street to street, anxious to fly that image which haunted him. His dress became neglected, and he wandered, as often exposed to the noon-day sun as to the mid-night damps. He was no longer to be recognized; at first he returned with evening to the house; but at last he laid him down to rest wherever fatigue overtook him. His sister, anxious for his safety, employed people to follow him; but they were soon distanced by him who fled from a pursuer swifter than any -- from thought. His conduct, however, suddenly changed. Struck with the idea that he left by his absence the whole of his friends, with a fiend amongst them, of whose presence they were unconscious, he determined to enter again into society, and watch him closely, anxious to forewarn, in spite of his oath, all whom Lord Ruthven approached with intimacy. But when he entered into a room, his haggard and suspicious looks were so striking, his inward shuddering so visible, that his sister was at last obliged to beg of him to abstain from seeking, for her sake, a society which affected him so strongly. When, however, remonstrance proved unavailing, the guardians thought proper to interpose, and, fearing that his mind was becoming alienated, they thought it high time to resume again that trust which had been before imposed upon them by Aubrey's parents.

Desirous of saving him from the injuries and sufferings he had daily encountered in his wanderings, and of preventing him from exposing to the general eye those marks of what they considered folly, they engaged a physician to reside in the house, and take constant care of him. He hardly appeared to notice it, so completely was his mind absorbed by one terrible subject. His incoherence became at last so great that he was confined to his chamber. There he would often lie for days, incapable of being roused. He had become emaciated, his eyes had attained a glassy lustre; -- the only sign of affection and recollection remaining displayed itself upon the entry of his sister; then he would sometimes start, and, seizing her hands, with looks that severely afflicted her, he would desire her not to touch him. "Oh, do not touch him -- if your love for me is aught, do not go near him!" When, however, she inquired to whom he referred, his only answer was, "True! true!" and again he sank into a state, whence not even she could rouse him. This lasted many months: gradually, however, as the year was passing, his incoherences became less frequent, and his mind threw off a portion of its gloom, whilst his guardians observed, that several times in the day he would count upon his fingers a definite number, and then smile.

The time had nearly elapsed, when, upon the last day of the year, one of his guardians entering his room, began to converse with his physician upon the melancholy circumstance of Aubrey's being in so awful a situation, when his sister was going next day to be married. Instantly Aubrey's attention was attracted; he asked anxiously to whom. Glad of this mark of returning intellect, of which they feared he had been deprived, they mentioned the name of the Earl of Marsden. Thinking this was a young Earl whom he had met with in society, Aubrey seemed pleased, and astonished them still more by his expressing his intention to be present at the nuptials, and desiring to see his sister. They answered not, but in a few minutes his sister was with him.

He was apparently again capable of being affected by the influence of her lovely smile; for he pressed her to his breast, and kissed her cheek, wet with tears, flowing at the thought of her brother's being once more alive to the feelings of affection. He began to speak with all his wonted warmth, and to congratulate her upon her marriage with a person so distinguished for rank and every accomplishment; when he suddenly perceived a locket upon her breast; opening it, what was his surprise at beholding the features of the monster who had so long influenced his life. He seized the portrait in a paroxysm of rage, and trampled it under foot. Upon her asking him why he thus destroyed the resemblance of her future husband, he looked as if he did not understand her; -- then seizing her hands, and gazing on her with a frantic expression of countenance, he bade her swear that she would never wed this monster, for he -- But he could not advance -- it seemed as if that voice again bade him remember his oath -- he turned suddenly round, thinking Lord Ruthven was near him but saw no one.

In the meantime the guardians and physician, who had heard the whole, and thought this was but a return of his disorder, entered, and forcing him from Miss Aubrey, desired her to leave him. He fell upon his knees to them, he implored, he begged of them to delay but for one day. They, attributing this to the insanity they imagined had taken possession of his mind endeavoured to pacify him, and retired.

Lord Ruthven had called the morning after the drawing-room, and had been refused with every one else. When he heard of Aubrey's ill health, he readily understood himself to be the cause of it; but when he learned that he was deemed insane, his exultation and pleasure could hardly be concealed from those among whom he had gained this information. He hastened to the house of his former companion, and, by constant attendance, and the pretence of great affection for the brother and interest in his fate, he gradually won the ear of Miss Aubrey. Who could resist his power? His tongue had dangers and toils to recount -- could speak of himself as of an individual having no sympathy with any being on the crowded earth, save with her to whom he addressed himself; -- could tell how, since he knew her, his existence had begun to seem worthy of preservation, if it were merely that he might listen her soothing accents; -- in fine, he knew so well how to use the serpent's art, or such was the will of fate, that he gained her affections. The title of the elder branch falling at length to him, he obtained an important embassy, which served as an excuse for hastening the marriage (in spite of her brother's deranged state), which was to take place the very day before his departure for the continent.

Aubrey, when he was left by the physician and his guardians, attempted to bribe the servants, but in vain. He asked for pen and paper; it was given him; he wrote a letter to his sister, conjuring her, as she valued her own happiness, her own honour, and the honour of those now in the grave, who once held her in their arms as their hope and the hope of their house, to delay but for a few hours that marriage, on which he denounced the most heavy curses. The servants promised they would deliver it; but giving it to the physician, he thought it better not to harass any more the mind of Miss Aubrey by, what he considered, the ravings of a maniac. Night passed on without rest to the busy inmates of the house; and Aubrey heard, with a horror that may more easily be conceived than described, the notes of busy preparation. Morning came, and the sound of carriages broke upon his ear.

Aubrey grew almost frantic. The curiosity of the servants at last overcame their vigilance; they gradually stole away, leaving him in the custody of an helpless old woman. He seized the opportunity, with one bound was out of the room, and in a moment found himself in the apartment where all were nearly assembled. Lord Ruthven was the first to perceive him: he immediately approached, and, taking his arm by force, hurried him from the room, speechless with rage.

When on the staircase, Lord Ruthven whispered in his ear -- "Remember your oath, and know, if not my bride to day, your sister is dishonoured. Women are frail!" So saying, he pushed him towards his attendants, who, roused by the old woman, had come in search of him. Aubrey could no longer support himself; his rage not finding vent, had broken a blood-vessel, and he was conveyed to bed. This was not mentioned to his sister, who was not present when he entered, as the physician was afraid of agitating her. The marriage was solemnized, and the bride and bridegroom left London.

Aubrey's weakness increased; the effusion of blood produced symptoms of the near approach of death. He desired his sister's guardians might be called, and when the midnight hour had struck, he related composedly what the reader has perused -- he died immediately after.

The guardians hastened to protect Miss Aubrey; but when they arrived, it was too late.

Lord Ruthven had disappeared, and Aubrey's sister had glutted the thirst of a VAMPYRE!

NEXT ATTRACTION

Books by
Philip J. Riley

CLASSIC HORROR FILMS
Frankenstein, the original 1931 shooting script
Bride of Frankenstein, the original 1935 shooting script
Son of Frankenstein, the original 1939 shooting script
Ghost of Frankenstein, the original 1942 shooting script
Frankenstein Meets the Wolf Man, the original 1943 shooting script
House of Frankenstein, the original 1944 shooting script
The Mummy, the original 1932 shooting script
The Mummy's Curse the original 1944 shooting script (as Editor in Chief)
The Wolf Man, the original 1941 shooting script
Dracula, the original 1931 shooting script
House of Dracula, the original 1945 shooting script

CLASSIC COMEDY FILMS
Abbott & Costello Meet Frankenstein, the original 1948 shooting script

CLASSIC SCIENCE FICTION
This Island Earth, the original 1955 shooting script
The Creature from the Black Lagoon, the original 1953 shooting script (editor-in-chief)

THE ACKERMAN ARCHIVES SERIES - LOST FILMS
The Reconstruction of London After Midnight, the original 1927 shooting script
The Reconstruction of A Blind Bargain, the original 1922 shooting script
The Reconstruction of The Hunchback of Notre Dame, the original 1923 shooting script
The Divine Woman by Gladys Unger, 1928 - (as editor)

CLASSIC SILENT FILMS
The Reconstruction of The Phantom of the Opera, the original 1925 shooting script
The Reconstruction of "London After Midnight" the original 1927 hooting script (2nd edition)

FILMONSTER SERIES - LOST SCRIPTS
James Whale's Dracula's Daughter, 1934
Cagliostro, The King of the Dead, 1932
Wolf Man vs. Dracula 1944
Lon Chaney as Dracula/Nosferatu
Robert Florey's Frankenstein 1931
War Eagles (with David Conover)
Karloff as The Invisible Man 1932
Lon Chaney as "The Man Who Laughs" 1924

MAGIMAGE FILMBOOKS
Thr Reconstruction of The Hunchback of Notre Dame - Revised edition
Horror of Dracula 1958
The Invisible Man by Gregory Wm. Mank (as Editor)

AS EDITOR
Countess Dracula by Carroll Borland
My Hollywood, when both of us were young by Patsy Ruth Miller
Mr. Technicolor - Herbert Kalmus
Famous Monster of Filmland #2 by Forrest J Ackerman
Frankenstein - A play, 1931 by John Balderston - (editor)
The Wizard of MGM by A. Arnold Gillespie (co-editor with Robert Welch)

FILM DOCUMENTARIES
A Thousand Faces - as contributor (Photoplay Productions)
Universal Horrors - as contributor (Photoplay Productions)

Mr. Riley has also contributed to 12 film related books by various authors
as well as numerous magazine articles and received the Count Dracula Society Award
and was inducted into Universal's Horror Hall of Fame and
won the Halloween Book Festival 2011 award in the horror category
and again won a Halloween Book Festival Award in 2012

www.ingramcontent.com/pod-product-compliance
Lightning Source LLC
Chambersburg PA
CBHW080435230426
43662CB00015B/2277